# The Unofficial BIG LEBOWSKI COCKTAIL BOOK

## Over 50 Mixed Drink Recipes Inspired by the Cult Classic

### André Darlington

### Illustrations by Jennifer Hines

EPIC INK

HEY, CAREFUL, MAN,
THERE'S A BEVERAGE HERE!
—The Dude

TO ALL FOR WHOM CASUALNESS RUNS DEEP.

# CONTENTS

# NEW INFORMATION HAS COME TO LIGHT

Maybe you are a hippie or a slacker. Perhaps you are an avant-garde artist, dancer, or porn producer. Maybe you are a nihilist, or unemployed. It could be that you enjoy mixed drinks that feature heavy cream. Alternatively, you could be a member of the Venice Beach bowling team on the prowl for a tipple to serve after practice. It's even imaginable that you are a Vietnam veteran of Polish extraction who has converted to Judaism and is searching for the right Shabbos medicinal nip. However it happened, however you got here, the book you now hold in your hands is the exact right one for you at this time and place.

But what, you may ask, is a Big Lebowski cocktail? First we need to understand the film. It's an ode to the noir genre, and Los Angeles, the setting for the movie, is a town of legendary noir writers such as Raymond Chandler, who gave us characters like Philip Marlowe.

But rather than being a hard-boiled antihero who drinks Scotch from his desk drawer, our particular unemployed (and unintentional) gumshoe, the Dude, tanks up on White Russians. With its case of mistaken identity, a reclusive millionaire, an eccentric femme fatale, and a ransom gone wrong, this is a classic LA mystery story all right—but one gone sunny, silly, and stoner. What's more, there are quirky characters and trippy scenes along the way. The inspiration for the drinks herein is the Dude and his circle of friends, but also the acquaintances and villains, witty dialogue, and the city of Los Angeles itself.

Modern cocktailing, often pretentiously called "craft" cocktailing, with its rules and regulations, may seem like the antithesis to the laid-back world celebrated in *The Big Lebowski*. Today's jigger-happy bartenders are admittedly more high-strung Walter Sobchak than chill Dude. But, then again, the cocktail revolution launched in the late '90s (incidentally, around the same time as the release of *The Big Lebowski*) was about cutting through bullsh**t. No more giant glasses filled with cheap booze and fast-melting ice. No more premade mixers. The cocktail revivalists asked: Why not make mixed drinks less cheap and dumb, and more enjoyable and artistic? Just like a layered Coen Brother film. It was a good idea, man. It still is.

In keeping with the film's tone, the drinks you'll find in this book are as lazy as possible while still remaining modern; the level of effort required is entirely up to you. With this book, you'll quickly become adept at that other zesty enterprise: cocktailing (actual zest required). So roll out your rug, cue the whale songs, fix yourself some liquid refreshment, and—above all—relax.

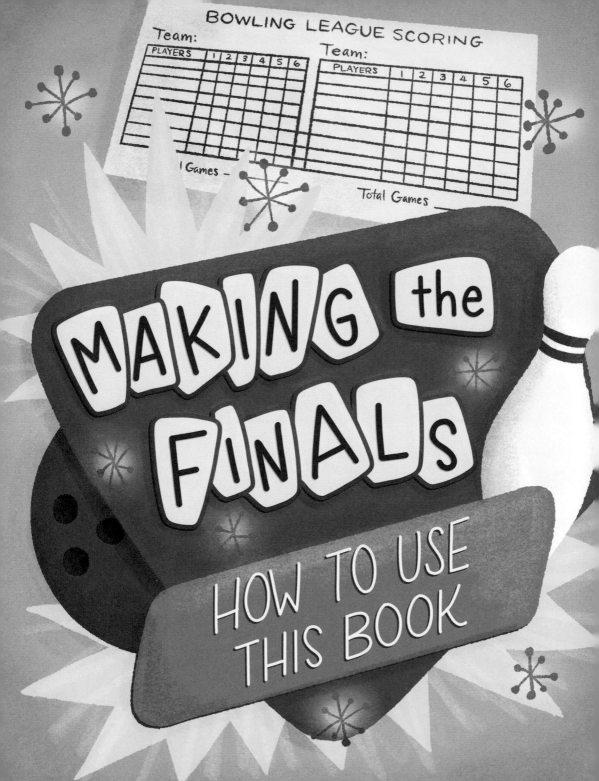

BOWLING LEAGUE SCORING

Team:

| PLAYERS | 1 | 2 | 3 | 4 | 5 | 6 |
|---------|---|---|---|---|---|---|
|  |  |  |  |  |  |  |
|  |  |  |  |  |  |  |
|  |  |  |  |  |  |  |
|  |  |  |  |  |  |  |
|  |  |  |  |  |  |  |
|  |  |  |  |  |  |  |

Games —

Team:

| PLAYERS | 1 | 2 | 3 | 4 | 5 | 6 |
|---------|---|---|---|---|---|---|
|  |  |  |  |  |  |  |
|  |  |  |  |  |  |  |
|  |  |  |  |  |  |  |
|  |  |  |  |  |  |  |
|  |  |  |  |  |  |  |
|  |  |  |  |  |  |  |

Total Games —

# MAKING the FINALs

## HOW TO USE THIS BOOK

*In these pages, you'll find over fifty cocktails* organized into three chapters based on level of ease and method of manufacture: pouring, shaking, and stirring. A fourth chapter covers important variations on the White Russian. For each drink entry, you will discover backstories, illuminating facts, and even an accompanying musical selection to set the mood.

Glassware recommendations are included in the recipes and feature common vessels such as rocks, highball, and wine glasses. When recipes call for a cocktail glass, this indicates a coupe or martini for serving up drinks.

All are single-serving beverages unless otherwise noted. Mixed into these chapter sections are a few communal large-format punches for gathering your bowling team. For more information on making any of the drinks in this book for a group, see page 18.

Drink ingredients are given using standard (imperial/American) measurements, but you can refer to the table opposite for handy-dandy metric conversions.

Like bowling, good cocktails require "staying within the lines," as Walter would say. Tips on how to do this correctly, without entering a world of pain, can be found on page 17. With some basic technique and helpful gear—and just a little practice—you, too, will reach the finals.

| FLUID OUNCES | CUPS/TABLESPOONS | METRIC |
|:---:|:---:|:---:|
| 16 ounces | 2 cups | 480 milliliters |
| 12 ounces | 1½ cups | 360 milliliters |
| 8 ounces | 1 cup | 240 milliliters |
| 6 ounces | ¾ cup | 180 milliliters |
| 5 ounces | 1 cup + 2 tablespoons | 150 milliliters |
| 4 ounces | ½ cup | 120 milliliters |
| 3 ounces | 6 tablespoons | 90 milliliters |
| 2 ounces | ¼ cup | 60 milliliters |
| 1 ounce | ⅛ cup/2 tablespoons | 30 milliliters |
| ¾ ounce | 1½ tablespoons | 22.5 milliliters |
| ½ ounce | 1 tablespoon | 15 milliliters |

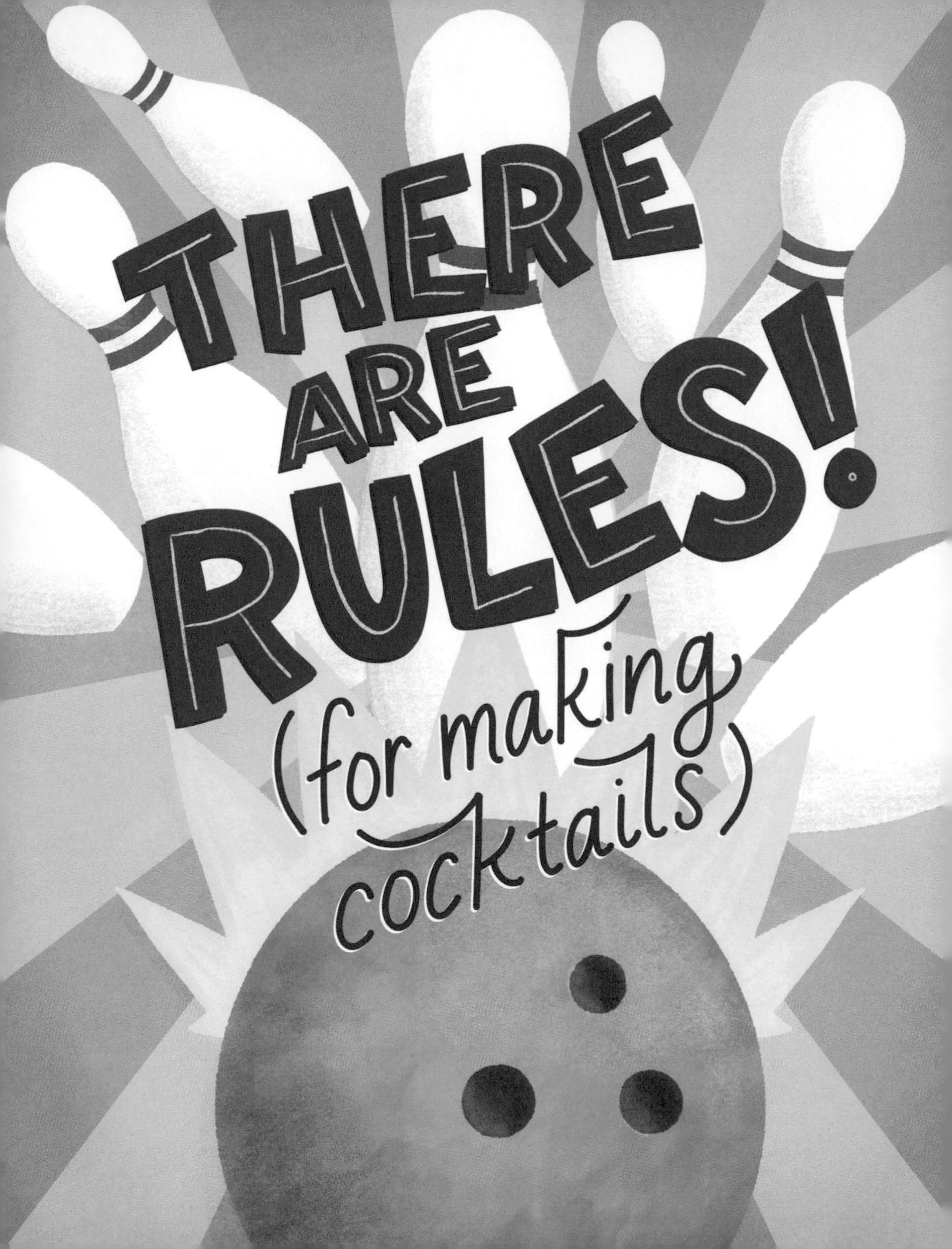
THERE ARE RULES!
(for making cocktails)

*As Walter Sobchak tells us, when a plan gets* too complex, that's when everything can go wrong. But a little planning goes a long way in making great cocktails.

**MEASURING** · Use a jigger to measure ingredients. This ensures you make a consistent, balanced drink every time—and you can recalibrate with precision if something is too sweet or too sour. You can always free-pour later if you really think you've nailed your recipe and technique.

**ICE & ICE TRAYS** · Ice is an integral part of cocktail making. Be sure to use fresh ice. Ice can take on "off" flavors from your freezer if stored too long. It also helps to use filtered water. Silicone ice trays will allow you to make perfect squares and large cubes.

**GARNISH** · Garnish isn't just for looks. A spritz of lemon zest over a drink adds aroma and flavor—and changes the cocktail. Have your garnish handy so you're not searching for it after you've made a drink.

**FRESH CITRUS** · Don't use bottled juice. Fresh citrus will enliven your cocktails immeasurably. See tool recommendations for citrus press (page 25).

**HOW TO RINSE A GLASS** · Add a barspoon of spirit to a glass. Then, tilt the glass and roll it to evenly distribute the spirit and coat the inside. Discard the extra liquid—or don't, depending on your preference.

**CREATING A SALT OR SUGAR RIM** · Run the edge of a citrus wedge along the lip of a glass so the juice moistens the rim. Invert the glass and dip it onto a plate of salt or sugar. Tap the glass a couple of times to remove the excess.

**CREATING CITRUS PEEL** · Using a y-shaped peeler, cut a swatch of skin from the outside of the citrus fruit. With a little practice, this will create thin, evenly cut peels every time.

**WHEN TO STIR** · Cocktails that are made up of spirits—think martinis and Manhattans—are stirred. Combine stirred cocktails and ice in a mixing glass and stir with a barspoon until the cocktail is chilled, at least 35 to 40 seconds.

**WHEN TO SHAKE** · When a cocktail recipe calls for citrus, eggs, or milk, combine the ingredients in a shaker with ice. Shake vigorously to emulsify the ingredients. To prevent ice shivs or other particles in the cocktail, strain the drink using a Hawthorne strainer (see page 25).

**HOW TO MUDDLE** · Drinks with citrus, sugar cubes, or herbs such as mint are sometimes muddled. When muddling herbs, use a wooden muddler (see page 25) to gently express the oils from the leaves—do not pulverize the herbs into tiny bits. Note: "Expressing" means squeezing the oils from citrus fruit peel.

**HOW TO BATCH COCKTAILS FOR A PARTY** · A useful trick for batching cocktails is to convert ounces in any cocktail recipe into cups.

# COMMON COCKTAIL RATIOS FOR CREATING YOUR OWN DRINKS

Cocktail recipes are often time-tested ratios that work. But after making a few hundred classics, you may be ready to strike out on your own. Two established ratios for making your own cocktails from scratch are below.

## THE 2:1:1

2 ounces base spirit

1 ounce sour (citrus)

1 ounce sweet liqueur (or simple syrup, recipe page 58)

Dash aromatics, such as bitters

## THE 3:2:1

3 ounces base spirit

2 ounces sweet or sour

1 ounce sweet or sour

# Really Tying Your Bar Together

## BOTTLES, PANTRY RECOMMENDATIONS, AND TOOLS

# BOTTLES

A well-stocked bar is something you build over time. Beginning with a few basic bottles, you can start to make drinks immediately and then add interesting liqueurs and spirits as you explore. Below is a list for a great starter bar.

## 12 Bottles to Get You Started

GIN

WHISKEY

TEQUILA

RUM

BRANDY

VODKA

CAMPARI

AMARO

COINTREAU

LUXARDO MARASCHINO LIQUEUR

SWEET VERMOUTH

DRY VERMOUTH

# PANTRY RECOMMENDATIONS

**BITTERS** · Angostura, Peychaud's, and orange bitters are all employed in classic cocktails and in this book—and are worth keeping on hand.

**OLIVES** · Spanish Manzanilla olives were long the standard in cocktails such as martinis. These days, Castelvetrano olives are appearing frequently at US bars.

**COCKTAIL ONIONS** · The venerable cocktail onion is most famous in the Gibson but also appears in Bloody Marys and other drinks that have a savory note.

**COCKTAIL CHERRIES** · Over the past twenty years, Amarena cherries have supplanted those fake-red-dye cocktail cherries. There are, however, a few brands that do make decent maraschino cherries, and they are worth seeking out.

**CLUB SODA** · Carbonated water, seltzer, and club soda are not as interchangeable as one might think. Club soda includes additives such as sodium and potassium that lend additional flavor to drinks.

**EGGS** · Fear not the raw egg; they make for incredible texture in mixed drinks. To prevent the shells from getting into your drink, always crack the egg on a counter surface and not on the edge of a glass. If you have a compromised immune system, consider using pasteurized eggs or powdered egg whites as an alternative; 2 teaspoons powder to 1 ounce water will yield a single white.

# ORGEAT

Orgeat is a cloudy almond-citrus syrup that was once consumed during summer—on its own or with liqueurs. Orgeat is available in cocktail stores and online, but it is easy (and less expensive) to make yourself. This quick recipe tastes fantastic and avoids squeezing almonds.

---

## SIMPLE ORGEAT RECIPE

*Makes 1 cup*

### INGREDIENTS

½ cup (100 g) sugar

Peel of ½ grapefruit

1 cup almond milk

8 drops almond extract

4 drops orange blossom water

### DIRECTIONS

In a medium resealable container, combine the sugar and grapefruit peel. Let macerate for 2 hours, or until the citrus oils have begun to soak into the sugar.

Add the almond milk and remove the peel.

Add the almond extract and orange blossom water, seal the container, and shake until the sugar dissolves. Orgeat will keep sealed in the refrigerator for 1 week.

# TOOLS

Crafting cocktails does not require a lot of fancy or expensive equipment, but there are a few items that will make your drinks mixing easier and improve quality.

**JIGGER** · Measuring precisely is a must for quality drinks. There are a number of options available on the market, and the OXO jigger is ideal for most home bartenders.

**BOSTON SHAKER** · The classic three-part shaker, often called a martini shaker, is not great for making most cocktails. It's often too small and the lid can get stuck when the metal cools from ice. The two-part Boston shaker is better. Originally composed of a metal tin and a pint glass, today the two parts are often both metal for safety. Two-part metal shakers are now widely available in kitchen stores and online.

**MIXING GLASSES** · Mixing glasses are used for all stirred drinks. Glasses have come down in price in the past few years. They are necessary for making stirred drinks correctly, but any vessel will work in a pinch.

**BARSPOON** · A barspoon is required to make properly stirred cocktails. One with enough heft at the end of the handle to crack ice is best, and they are widely available in kitchen stores and online.

**STRAINERS** · There are two styles of cocktail strainers: Hawthorne and julep. Hawthorne strainers are employed for shaken drinks, while julep strainers are used for stirred cocktails. If you are in doubt, buy a Hawthorne, which works just fine for both purposes.

**CITRUS JUICER** · Hand juicers are great for small amounts, but it is good to have a larger juicer with a reservoir. It may be worth investing in a quality juicer if you are making a lot of drinks for cocktail parties.

**ICE & ICE TRAYS** · Ice is a hugely important ingredient in cocktails and can be up to 25% of the volume of the final drink once shaken or stirred. It should be fresh, so use filtered or bottled water to ensure that natural, clean taste. Tip: To get rid of cloudiness and give your ice a glass-like clarity, boil the water and let cool before adding to molds and freezing. Purchase a few silicone trays to get those large, impressive cubes or spheres.

**Y-PEELER** · A y-peeler, sometimes called a Swiss peeler, is the ideal tool for citrus skin.

**MUDDLER** · A muddler should be made of nonstained, nonreactive wood. Steer clear of paint, plastic, or metal.

# GLASSWARE

No special glassware is required to enjoy a good drink. However, the average size for a proper cocktail is small when poured into commonly available glassware. If you do acquire cocktail-specific glasses, your first choice will likely be to invest in a set of coupe glasses—sometimes called champagne glasses—which are now widely available online. The best size for these is between 4 and 6 ounces. Additionally, good highball and rocks glasses can improve presentation.

# OTHER PREPARATION ITEMS

CUTTING BOARD

PARING KNIFE

BOTTLE OPENER

WINE KEY

SQUEEZE BOTTLES
(FOR CITRUS JUICE)

MICROPLANE

FUNNEL

LARGE-FORMAT
ICE CUBE TRAYS

ICE BUCKET

ICE SCOOP

HAND TOWELS

COCKTAIL PICKS

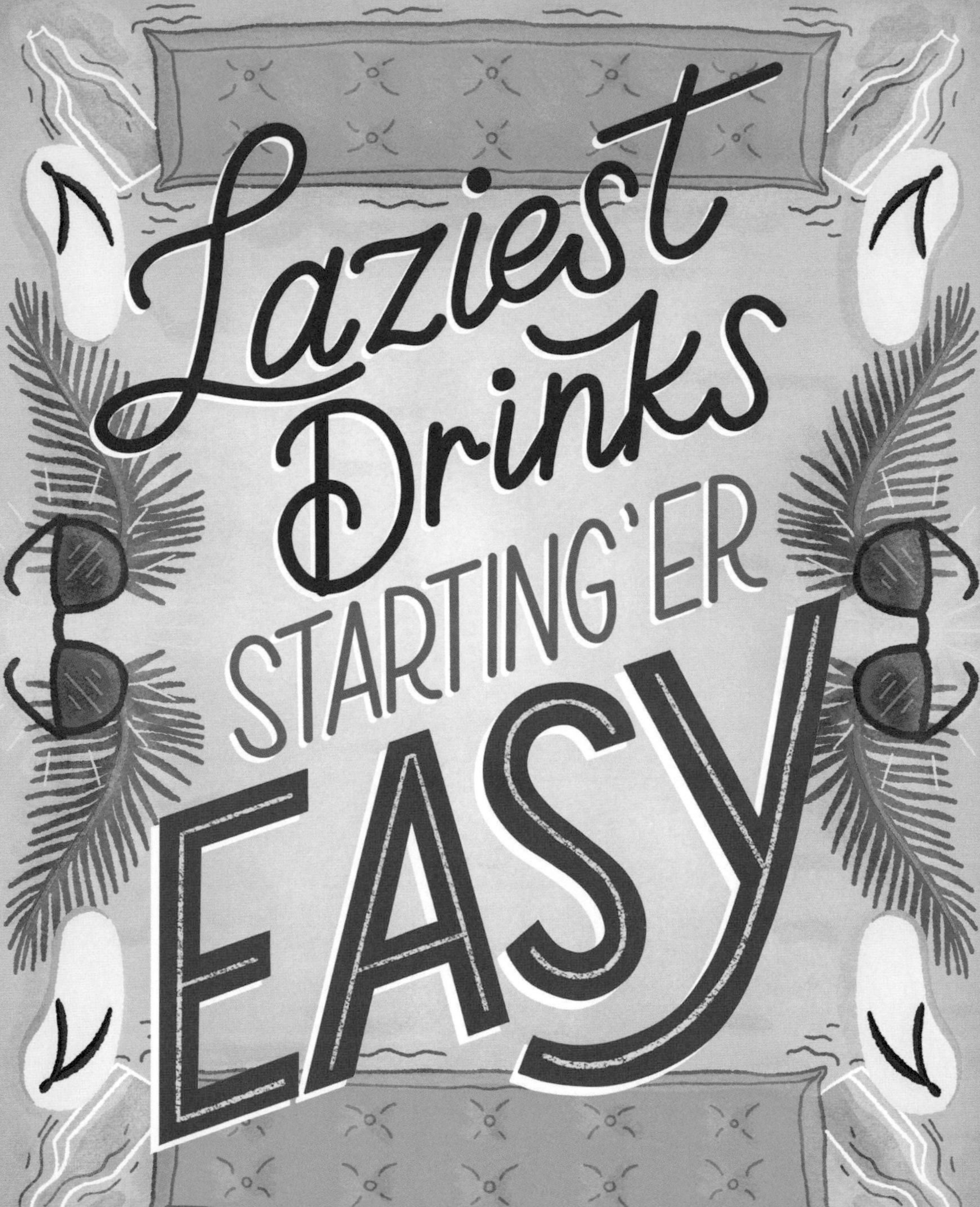
Laziest Drinks
STARTING'ER
EASY

*The cocktails in this chapter are in the running* for some of the laziest worldwide. Let's put it this way: if you can lift a bottle and pour its contents into a glass, you're in business. OK, maybe a single quick stir—you get the idea. But make no mistake, some of the best drinks in the world are built in the glass without fuss—including the famed White Russian (page 129). This section includes cocktails that are both perfect for starting a gathering and mixing up for yourself on a weeknight. You will find a number of drinks that will be your new casual go-tos as well as a few riffs on champagne cocktails, in case you need to invoke the royal we. For these sippers, note that while champagne is great, crémant or a nice dry prosecco will also do the trick.

# TUMBLEWEED

Open scene: A lone tumbleweed crosses a desert expanse and reaches the vast city of Los Angeles where it . . . heads down Hollywood Boulevard to the beach. Does the tumbleweed represent the Dude, who also wanders wherever the wind blows? A cowboy, played by actor Sam Elliott, narrates the stupefying tale, inviting us into the story of a man—and he's talking about the Dude here, a true sagebrush bohemian—who is "the man for his time and place."

## SAGE SIMPLE SYRUP

1 cup water

1 cup (200 g) sugar

20 sage leaves

## COCKTAIL

2 ounces bourbon whiskey

½ ounce fresh lemon juice

½ ounce Sage Simple Syrup

4 ounces club soda

Sage leaf, for garnish

## DIRECTIONS

To make the sage simple syrup: Bring the water to a boil, then remove from the heat.

Add the sugar and stir to dissolve. Add the sage leaves and let the mixture steep for 30 minutes.

Strain and store in the refrigerator in an airtight container for up to 2 weeks.

To make the cocktail: Combine the whiskey, lemon juice, and sage simple syrup in a rocks or highball glass with ice and top with the club soda.

Garnish with a sage leaf.

*Song Pairing*
"TUMBLING TUMBLEWEED"
by Sons of the Pioneers

# TUMBLEWEED

# WHERE'S BUNNY?

Bunny Lebowski, young trophy wife of the Big Lebowski, is missing. Has she been kidnapped? Has she cleverly kidnapped herself? Every epic plot needs an inciting incident to set the hero's journey in motion; ours happens to be the disappearance of a party girl named Bunny (played by actress Tara Reid). Start any party with this ode to green nail polish and poolside repose, a champagne cocktail ideal for welcoming guests. Pro tip: Cool the Midori and vodka in the freezer before constructing the cocktail.

## INGREDIENTS

¾ ounce vodka

¾ ounce Midori

5 ounces sparkling wine

## DIRECTIONS

Combine the vodka, Midori, and sparkling wine in a champagne flute or wineglass.

*Song Pairing*

"VIVA LAS VEGAS" by ZZ Top

### Dude Fact

In the movie's script, Bunny is listed as Fawn Gunderson, creating a possible link to Marge Gunderson from the film *Fargo*. Moorhead, Minnesota—where Fawn is from—is also the twin city of Fargo, North Dakota.

# THE ROYAL WE

The Dude's close friend Walter Sobchak can't help but involve himself in the transfer of ransom money to Bunny's kidnappers (or botch the job, as the case may be). The Dude was supposed to do it alone. When the Dude slips in the retelling of the incident to the Big Lebowski, he invokes the majestic plural. At this moment, the Dude has truly reached peak Dudeness. Celebrate with an equally sovereign cocktail. Often, the word royal or royale is employed in cocktail names to indicate the presence of champagne, such as in a kir royale. We approve of this usage.

## INGREDIENTS

1 ounce vanilla vodka

1 ounce Kahlúa

4 ounces sparkling wine

## DIRECTIONS

Combine the vodka, Kahlúa, and sparkling wine in a champagne flute or wineglass.

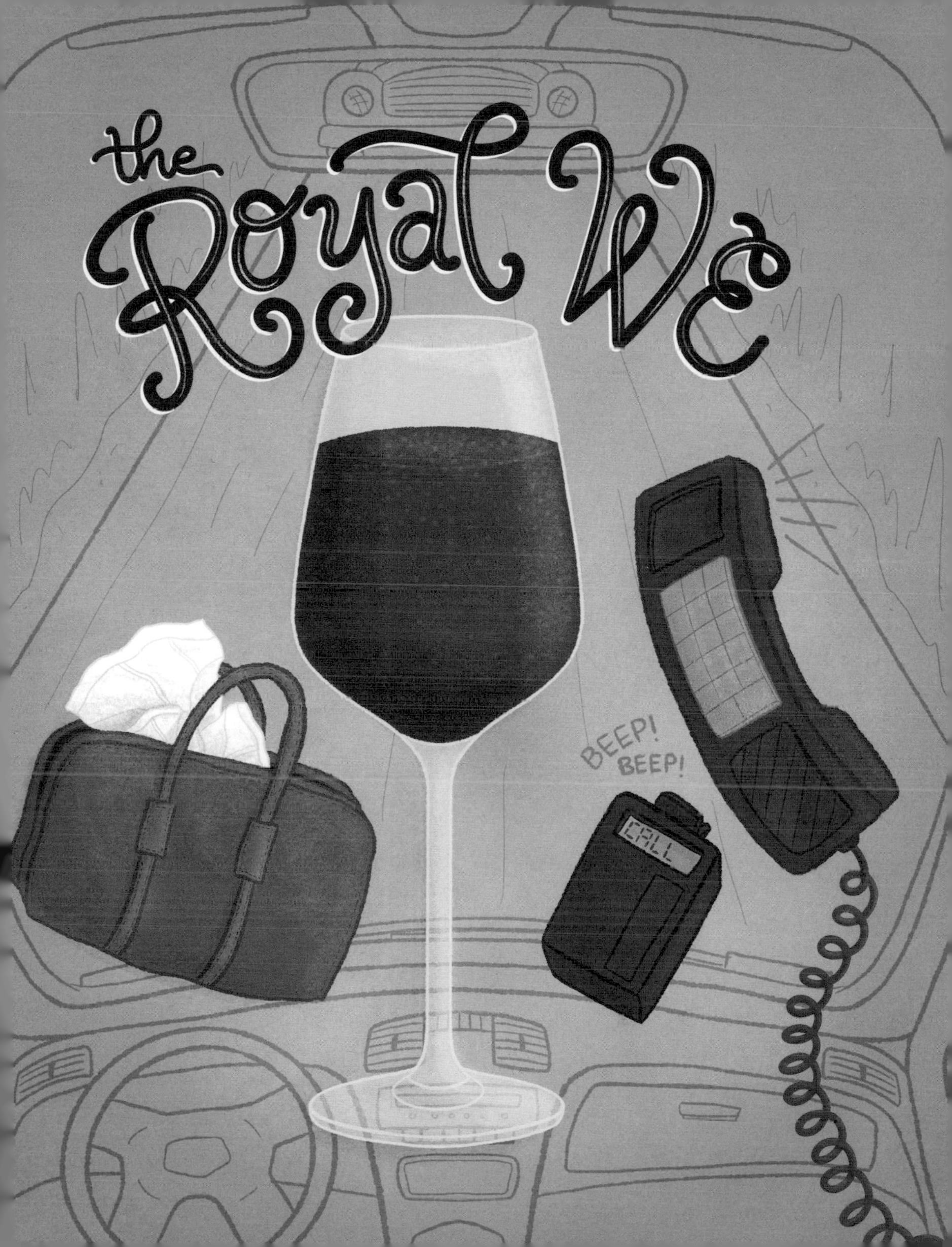
the Royal We
BEEP! BEEP!
CALL

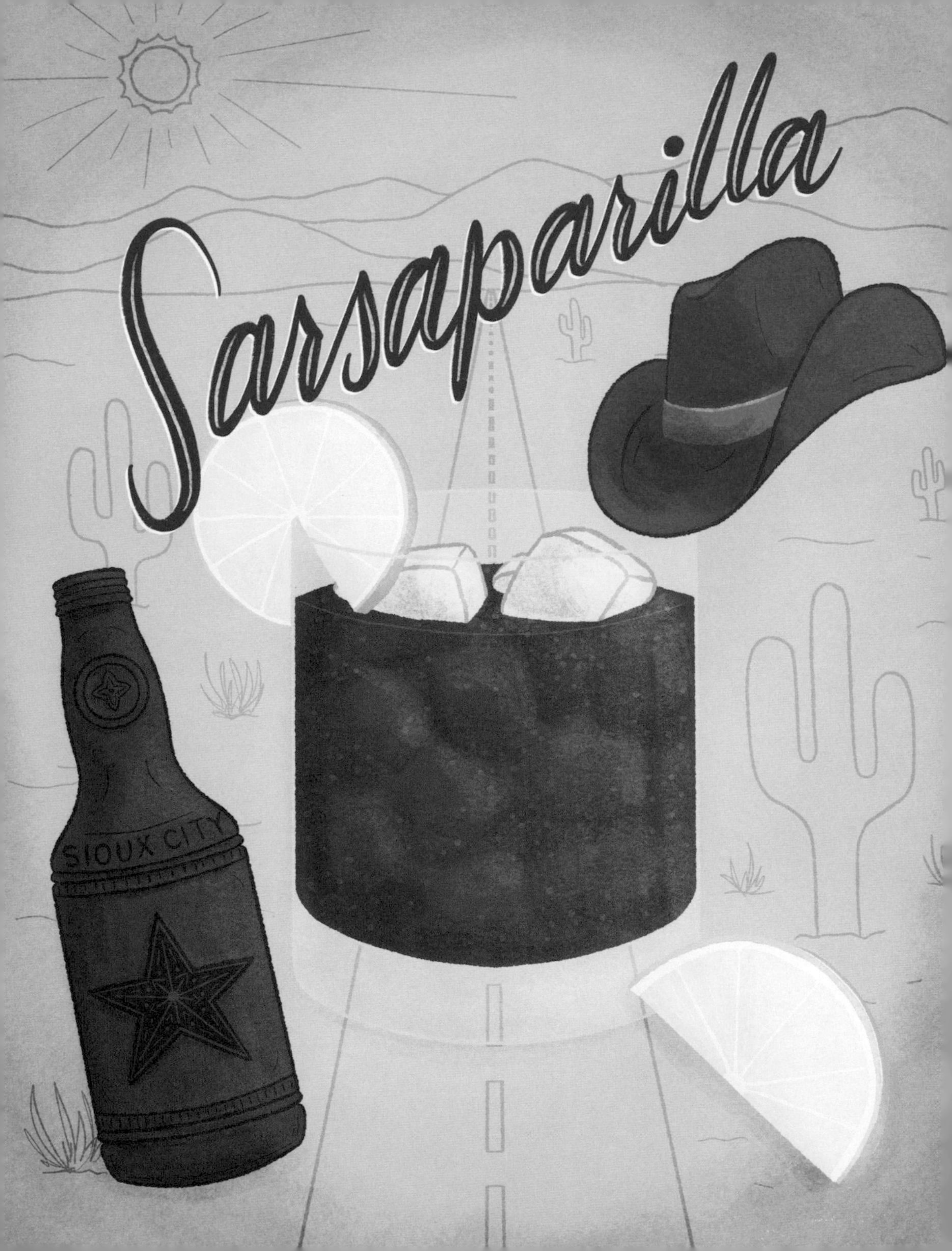
Sarsaparilla
SIOUX CITY

# SARSAPARILLA

Sioux City Sarsaparilla? That's a good one. Made with whiskey, a drop of citrus, and bitters, this soda-based cocktail makes for a mighty fine libation any tumbleweed will enjoy. Popular among cowboys in the nineteenth century, sarsaparilla was used as a remedy for skin and blood problems. The taste is similar to root beer, and the name derives from the Spanish *zarzaparrilla*, *zarza* meaning "bramble," or tumbleweed. See what the Coen Brothers did there? Peychaud's bitters are important in any cocktailer's arsenal and would likely have been the last bitters available (in New Orleans) before hitting the open road out West.

## INGREDIENTS

2 ounces bourbon whiskey

6 ounces sarsaparilla soda

Squeeze of ½ lemon

Dash Peychaud's bitters

## DIRECTIONS

Combine the whiskey, soda, lemon juice, and bitters in a highball glass filled with ice.

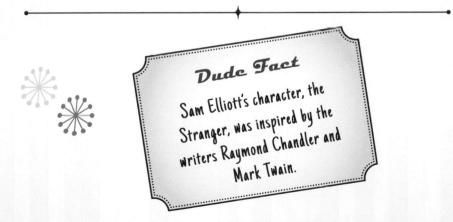

### Dude Fact

Sam Elliott's character, the Stranger, was inspired by the writers Raymond Chandler and Mark Twain.

# THE SOBCHAK

Walter Sobchak: Fifty-three years old. Overweight. Vietnam veteran. Divorced. Polish Catholic converted to Judaism. Does not bowl on Shabbos (Saturday). Best friend of the Dude. As both a Pole and Jew, Sobchak is a fan of *slivovitz*, or fruit brandy. While slivovitz is made from plums, the spirit is technically a kind of *pálinka* (Eastern European fruit brandy), which comes in many flavors, from apricot to pear. Any fruit brandy will work well, although the true Sobchak is sliv and ginger beer (with the addition of bitters for health reasons on Shabbos).

## INGREDIENTS

1¾ ounces fruit brandy, preferably slivovitz

6 ounces ginger beer

2 dashes Angostura bitters

## DIRECTIONS

Combine the brandy, ginger beer, and bitters in a highball glass with ice.

# THE
# SOBCHAK

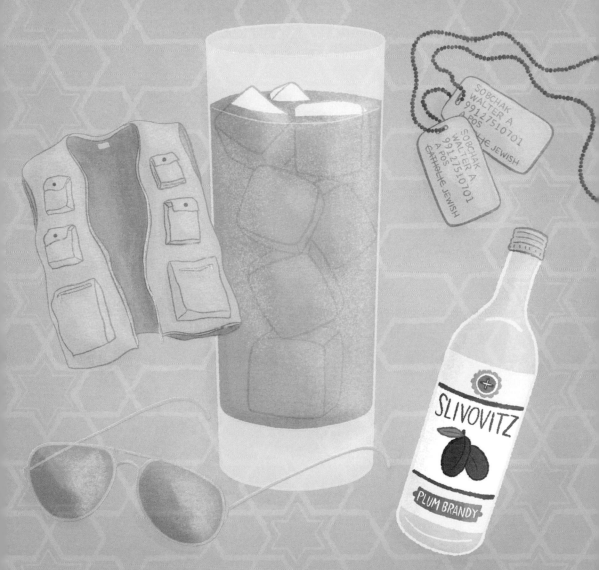

# KNOX OX HARRINGTON

GALLERY GUIDE

THE VENICE BIENNALE ART GUIDE

# KNOX HARRINGTON

Petulant layabout Knox Harrington is a video artist who assists
Maude Lebowski in her Carolee Schneemann–inspired endeavors.
For him, the world-famous art fair that is the Venice Biennale is his
Christmas, Olympics, and a speed-dating event all rolled into one.
Bellinis—white peach and prosecco—are the Biennale's signature
cocktail. But for Harrington, these are far too pedestrian and boring.
Rossinis—strawberry and prosecco—are so much livelier. He adds a
cocky dose of bitterness with Campari.

## STRAWBERRY PUREE

2 cups (290 g) fresh strawberries

## COCKTAIL

1 ounce strawberry puree

¾ ounce Campari

4 ounces prosecco

## DIRECTIONS

To make the strawberry puree: Add
the strawberries to a blender or food
processor and puree until smooth.

NOTE: IF YOU WANT TO GIVE YOUR PUREE
AN EXTRA KICK, TRY ADDING LEMON JUICE,
BASIL LEAVES, PEPPER, OR SALT, ALL TO YOUR
SPECIFIC TASTE.

To make the cocktail: Combine the
strawberry puree, Campari, and
prosecco in a champagne flute.

*Song Pairing*
"WE VENERATE THY CROSS"
by the Rustavi Choir

# KARL HUNGUS

A former porn star, Karl Hungus (a.k.a. Uli Kunkel) is now the leader of a group of German nihilists. A man of many talents, he was also once a member of the German pop band Autobahn. When Bunny tells Hungus that she is going to Palm Springs, Karl—ever the opportunist—fakes her kidnapping and extorts the Big Lebowski for a million dollars. This glittery German porn star–inspired number is ever popular with the gold-digging Hunguses among us. Especially delightful under soft lighting. Logjammin'!

## INGREDIENTS

½ ounce Goldschläger

½ ounce Grand Marnier

5 ounces sparkling wine

## DIRECTIONS

Combine the Goldschläger, Grand Marnier, and sparkling wine in a champagne flute.

*Song Pairing*

"TRAFFIC BOOM"
by Piero Piccioni

# LET'S GO BOWLING

Beer has a long and enduring history as a mixed-drink ingredient. Think shandies, micheladas, and black velvets. Beer brings the mellow to the party, but it also provides great body. Here, ginger liqueur and bitters offer an extra pop of flavor—and alcohol—to any beer for a nearly ready-made cocktail that will raise eyebrows. Fabulous stuff, man.

## INGREDIENTS

12 ounces light beer

1 ounce ginger liqueur, such as Domaine de Canton

Juice of ¼ lime

Dash Angostura bitters

## DIRECTIONS

Combine the beer, ginger liqueur, lime juice, and bitters in a pint glass.

Song Pairing

"THE MAN IN ME" by Bob Dylan

# THE KERABATSOS

An homage to bowling friend Donny Kerabatsos's Greek heritage, this cocktail is the gin and juice of the Star Lanes bowling world. We will forever remember Donny for shutting up, but, more importantly, for throwing rocks like a god. Those bowling pins never had a chance. The Kerabatsos is best consumed out of a red Solo cup but can be served in finer glassware if another clean receptacle is available.

### INGREDIENTS

1½ ounces ouzo

4 ounces fresh orange juice

### DIRECTIONS

Combine the ouzo and orange juice in a rocks glass with ice.

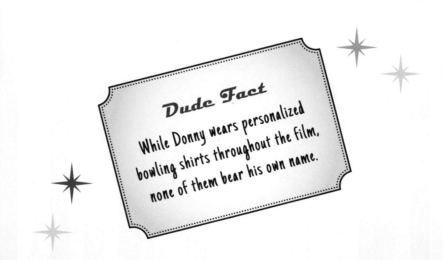

*Dude Fact*

While Donny wears personalized bowling shirts throughout the film, none of them bear his own name.

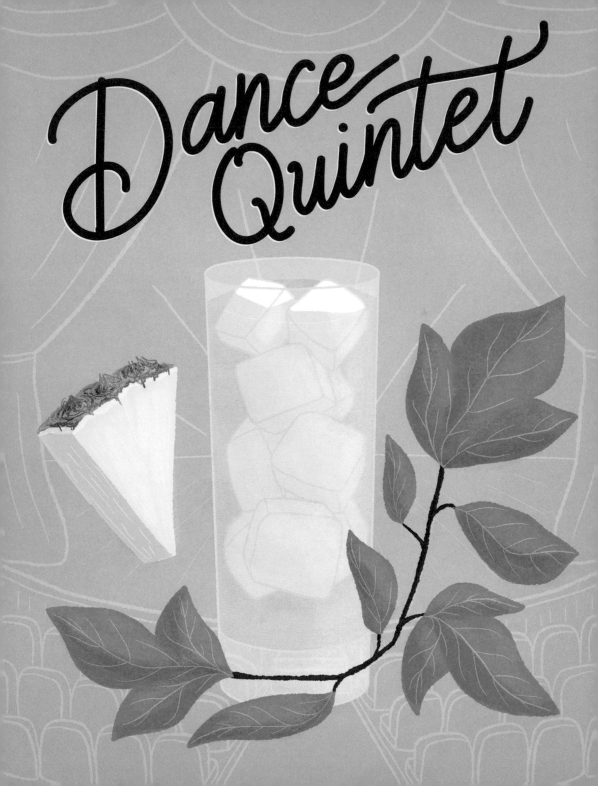

# DANCE QUINTET

The Dude's landlord, Marty, is part of a dance ensemble, and we learn that he has finally found a venue in which to perform his dance cycle. Marty would love it if the Dude would drop by and give him notes on the performance. When the Dude shows up, Marty is dancing to the second movement of Mussorgsky's "Pictures at an Exhibition." Do yourself a favor and look up the portrait of Mussorgsky by Ilya Repin on the internet; it is the Dude. Enjoy this dancer-friendly kombucha cocktail while jotting down performance notes.

## INGREDIENTS

1½ ounces vodka

2 ounces fruit kombucha

2 ounces fresh pineapple juice

## DIRECTIONS

Combine the vodka, kombucha, and pineapple juice in a highball glass with ice.

*Song Pairing*

"PICTURES AT AN EXHIBITION: GNOMUS"
by Modest Mussorgsky

# THE POMERANIAN

Despite being divorced from his wife, Cynthia, for five years, Walter still takes care of her Pomeranian while she vacations with her boyfriend. It is an arrangement that confuses everyone except Walter. He loves Cynthia, and the Pomeranian can stay in its pet carrier while he bowls. Additionally, he does not have to rent it shoes or buy it a beer, and it doesn't take anyone's turn. No problemo! Descended from mighty sled dogs, Pomeranians have a big-dog personality in a miniature body—just like this cocktail, which packs an outsize punch.

## INGREDIENTS

2 ounces applejack

1½ ounces pomegranate juice

3 ounces club soda

Dash Angostura bitters

## DIRECTIONS

Combine the applejack, pomegranate juice, club soda, and bitters in a rocks glass with ice.

*Dude Fact*

The dog in the film isn't a Pomeranian at all but a Yorkshire terrier.

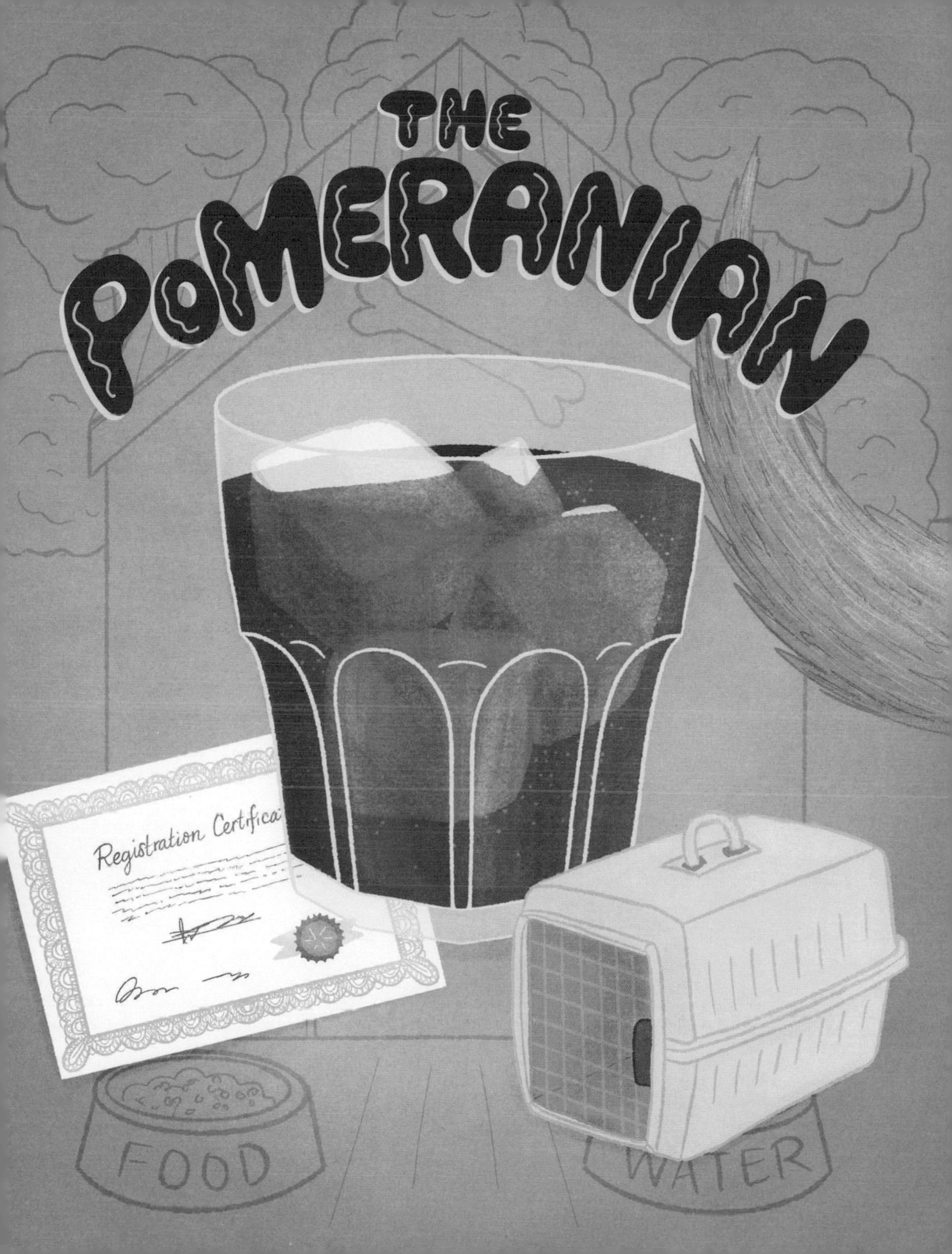
THE POMERANIAN
Registration Certifica
FOOD
WATER

# I AM THE WALRUS

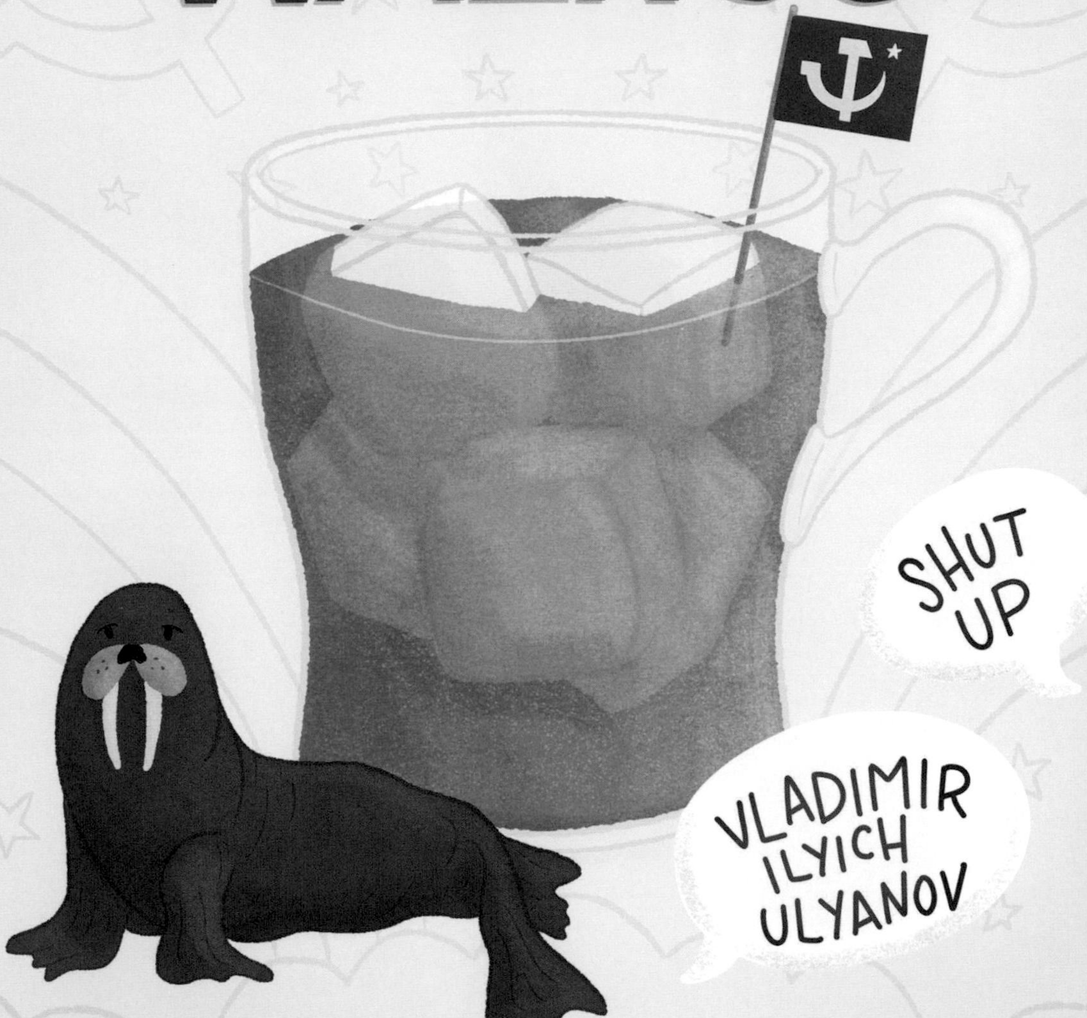

# I AM THE WALRUS

Poor bowling buddy Donny. When he mistakes "Lenin" for "Lennon" in a conversation between the Dude and Walter, he begins intoning the lyrics from a Beatles' song. At the very least, we owe him (and his memory) this Moscow mule variation, best served in a coffee mug à la the Dude. The amaro here gives the classic a little Donny-esque twist. Huh? Shut up!

## INGREDIENTS

1½ ounces vodka

½ ounce amaro, such as Averna

6 ounces ginger beer

## DIRECTIONS

Combine the vodka, amaro, and ginger beer in a mug or highball glass with ice.

*Song Pairing*

"I AM THE WALRUS"
by The Beatles

# OVER THE LINE!

Was bowling rival Smokey really over the line? We'll never know. What we do know is that Walter loses his cool and pulls a gun. If Smokey's toe did slip over the line and caused a foul, the score must be marked zero. There are rules! Fun fact: the Cohen Brothers searched for a bowling alley location that featured manual scoring, already a rarity in Los Angeles in the late '90s. Hollywood Star Lanes fit the bill, but the popular alley was soon razed to make room for an elementary school. Just please remember which side of the line to stay on. This isn't 'Nam.

## INGREDIENTS

¼ ounce mezcal

1 sugar cube

2 dashes orange bitters

2 dashes Angostura bitters

2 ounces aged rum

## DIRECTIONS

Rinse a rocks glass with the mezcal.

Add the sugar cube and muddle it with the bitters.

Add the rum and a large ice cube.

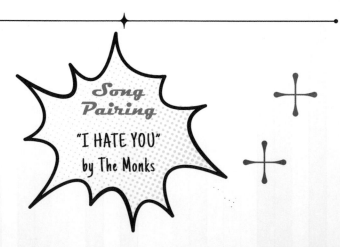

Song Pairing

"I HATE YOU" by The Monks

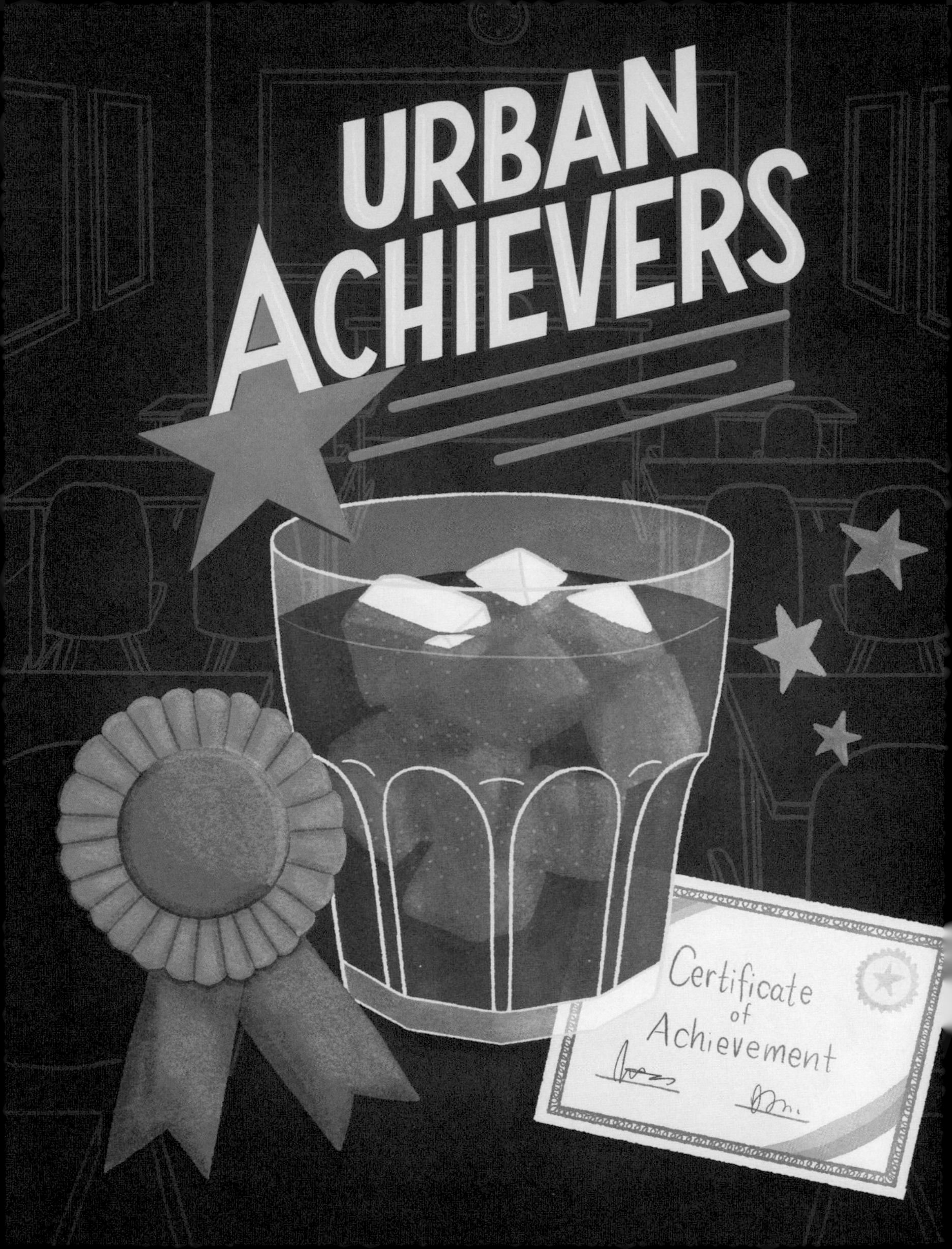
URBAN ACHIEVERS
Certificate of Achievement

# URBAN ACHIEVERS

Toast to the Little Lebowski Urban Achievers with this country club–inspired cranberry cocktail. It must gall the Dude a bit that the Big Lebowski's urban achievers are also "little" Lebowskis—and that rather than slacking and bowling, they are accomplishing things. We are, indeed, proud of all of them. Pinkies out.

## INGREDIENTS

1½ ounces vanilla vodka

2 ounces cranberry juice

4 ounces club soda

## DIRECTIONS

Combine the vodka, cranberry juice, and club soda in a rocks glass filled with ice.

# VENICE BEACH LEAGUE
## Serves 6 to 8

Almost as famous as the Philadelphia Fish House Punch, the Venice Beach League packs a similar wallop. The VBL, as it is lovingly known, is rumored to have been consumed by Bob Dylan once in the '70s. Mix up a batch anytime the bowling buddies are gathered and enjoy its strong charms. But be sure to pace yourself or you'll have a mighty hangover.

### SIMPLE SYRUP

1 cup water

1 cup (200 g) sugar

### COCKTAIL

12 ounces bourbon whiskey

¾ cup grapefruit juice

½ cup simple syrup

6 cans (12 ounces each) lager-style beer

Lemon slices, for garnish

### DIRECTIONS

To make the simple syrup: Bring the water to a boil, then remove from the heat.

Add the sugar and stir to dissolve.

Store in the refrigerator in an airtight container for up to 2 weeks.

To make the cocktail: In a large punch bowl with ice, combine the whiskey, grapefruit juice, simple syrup, and beer.

Stir to combine and serve in individual beer glasses garnished with lemon slices.

### Dude Fact

Rolling Stones producer Allen Klein waived the fee for the use of the song "Dead Flowers" because he thought the scene in which the Dude expresses his hatred for the Eagles was so funny.

# VENICE BEACH LEAGUE

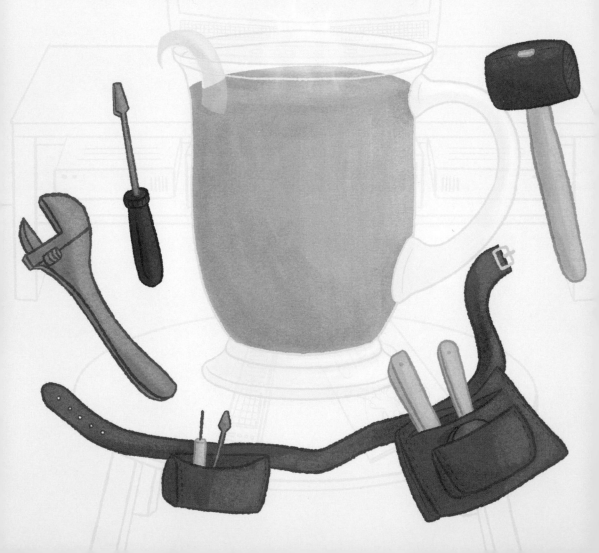

# LOGJAMMIN'

Honor the slammin' performances by actors Karl Hungus and Bunny Lebowski in the film *Logjammin'* with this inviting winter warmer. The movie plot hinges on the premise that a German handyman has been dispatched to fix a woman's cable (represented by the lemon peel in this drink). In a surprise twist of fate, Bunny's friend Shari comes over to use the shower at the exact same time. What will happen?!

## INGREDIENTS

1 ounce bourbon whiskey

1 ounce maple syrup

¼ ounce fresh lemon juice

8 ounces hot water

Lemon peel, for garnish

## DIRECTIONS

Combine the whiskey, maple syrup, and lemon juice in a glass or mug.

Add the hot water and stir.

Garnish with a lemon peel.

### Dude Fact

The character Shari in *Logjammin'* is played by Asia Carrera, who at the time was one of the world's most famous porn stars.

*Just as there are rules in bowling, there are rules* for making cocktails. One such rule is that mixed drinks are to be shaken when they contain citrus, eggs, or dairy. Shaking emulsifies and aerates the drink while simultaneously chilling it down and providing proper dilution. Because many shaken drinks include citrus juices, they tend to be lighter and more refreshing—think daiquiris and margaritas—than their stirred spirituous cousins. In this chapter, expect Bunny Lebowski's poolside sipper as well as Jackie Treehorn's beach party starter.

# RANSOM COURIER

After calling the Dude a bum and throwing him out of his mansion, the Big Lebowski sends his servant Brandt to kindly ask the Dude to be his bagman for a ransom delivery. Why would the Dude accept such an offer? Because he'll get an easy $20,000 if he acts as a ransom courier! Enjoy this Southern California riff on the venerable Airmail, a drink created to honor delivery. The first versions of this cocktail even sported a postage stamp for garnish. But remember: no funny stuff.

## INGREDIENTS

1½ ounces white rum

¾ ounce Cointreau

¾ ounce fresh lime juice

1 ounce sparkling wine, to top

Orange twist, for garnish

## DIRECTIONS

Using a shaker, shake the rum, Cointreau, and lime juice with ice.

Strain into a cocktail glass, top with the sparkling wine, and garnish with an orange twist.

*Song Pairing*

"RUN THROUGH THE JUNGLE"
by Creedence Clearwater Revival

OCCASIONAL
ACID
FLASHBACK

# OCCASIONAL ACID FLASHBACK

When asked by Maude what he does for recreation, the Dude shares his top three pastimes: bowling, driving around, and occasional acid flashbacks. He sure had a bit of fun with psychedelics back in the day. What exactly is a flashback? HPPD, or hallucinogen persisting perception disorder, is the clinical term for seeing trippy, weird things like flashes of color, geometric phenomena, afterimages, and inaccurate perceptions of movement. Alternatively, try this drink.

## INGREDIENTS

1 ounce coconut rum, such as Malibu

1 ounce aged rum

2 ounces fresh pineapple juice

½ ounce fresh lime juice

1 ounce Coco López

## DIRECTIONS

Using a shaker, shake the rums, pineapple juice, and lime juice.

Strain into a rocks glass with a large ice cube.

Using a barspoon, drizzle the Coco López over the top of the drink.

*Song Pairing*

"JUST DROPPED IN (TO SEE WHAT CONDITION MY CONDITION WAS IN)"

by Kenny Rogers & The First Edition

# BOWLING WITH JESUS

Jesus Quintana is more legend than man. He is an institution in a monogrammed purple jumpsuit. What's more, he is a formidable opponent to the Dude's bowling team. Oh, and he can really lick a bowling ball. Nobody f**ks with da Jesus! This drink is deep purple, so be sure to color coordinate by wearing the appropriate attire.

## INGREDIENTS

1½ ounces blanco tequila

½ ounce maraschino liqueur

½ ounce Chambord

¾ ounce fresh lemon juice

Cocktail cherry, for garnish

## DIRECTIONS

Using a shaker, shake the tequila, maraschino liqueur, Chambord, and lemon juice with ice and strain into a cocktail glass.

Garnish with a cherry.

*Song Pairing*
"HOTEL CALIFORNIA"
by Gipsy Kings

*Dude Fact*
For the character of Jesus, actor John Turturro created the bulge in his pants with a bag of birdseed.

# Tai the Room Together

# TAI THE ROOM TOGETHER

The Dude's rug really tied the room together. But be forewarned that there's wordplay here—because the Dude also practices his Tai Chi exercises on the very rug that ties his room together. Despite its exotic name, the mai tai is a classic cocktail hailing from California and was likely created by Victor Bergeron at Trader Vic's in Oakland. There are a number of versions of the mai tai, and this Duder tai is a straightforward take on the original that is sure to please.

## INGREDIENTS

1 ounce dark rum

1 ounce light rum

1 ounce orgeat (recipe page 23)

¾ ounce fresh lime juice

½ ounce heavy cream

## DIRECTIONS

Using a shaker, shake the rums, orgeat, and lime juice with ice and pour into a rocks glass.

Top with the heavy cream.

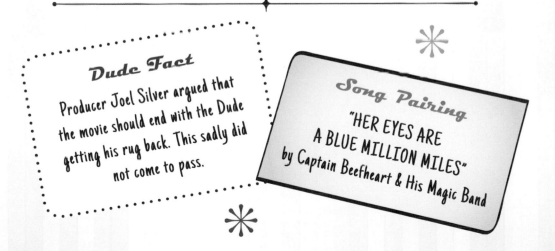

### Dude Fact

Producer Joel Silver argued that the movie should end with the Dude getting his rug back. This sadly did not come to pass.

### Song Pairing

"HER EYES ARE A BLUE MILLION MILES" by Captain Beefheart & His Magic Band

# BUNNY LEBOWSKI

Bunny Lebowski is very . . . free-spirited. When we first meet her lounging poolside and painting her toenails electric green, she is drinking a blue Hawaii—complete with a pineapple-themed straw. Only later do we learn that Bunny is Fawn Knutson, a simple girl from Minnesota who owes porn producer Jackie Treehorn money. So tasty, though!

## INGREDIENTS

¾ ounce vanilla vodka

¾ ounce light rum

½ ounce blue curaçao

3 ounces fresh pineapple juice

½ ounce fresh lime juice

Fresh pineapple wedge, for garnish

## DIRECTIONS

Using a shaker, shake the vodka, rum, blue curaçao, pineapple juice, and lime juice with ice and pour into a hurricane or highball glass.

Garnish with a pineapple wedge.

*Song Pairing*

"MUCHA MUCHACHA"
by Esquivel!

*Dude Fact*

The other actress considered by the Coen Brothers to play Bunny Lebowski was none other than Charlize Theron.

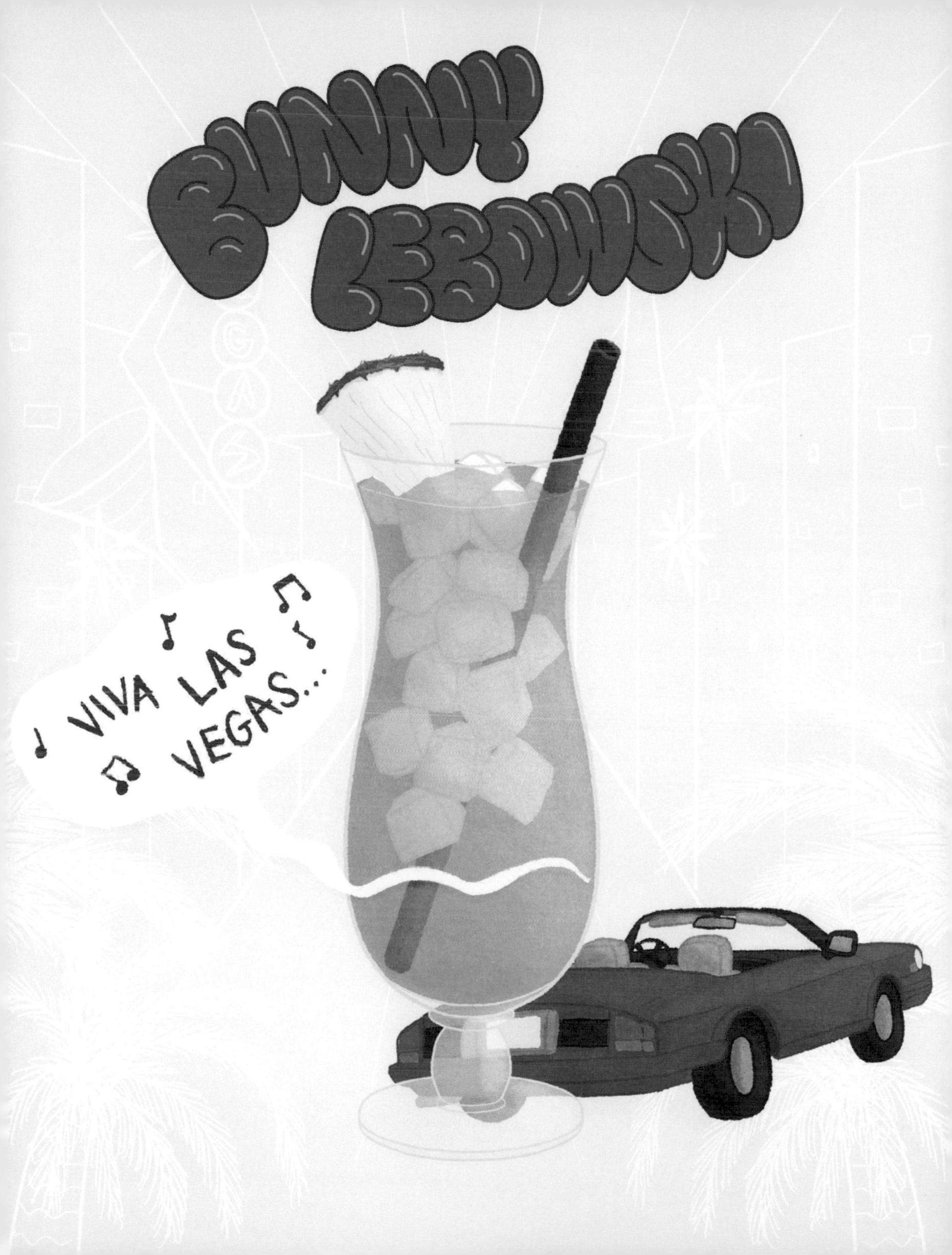
BUNNY LEBOWSKI
VIVA LAS VEGAS...

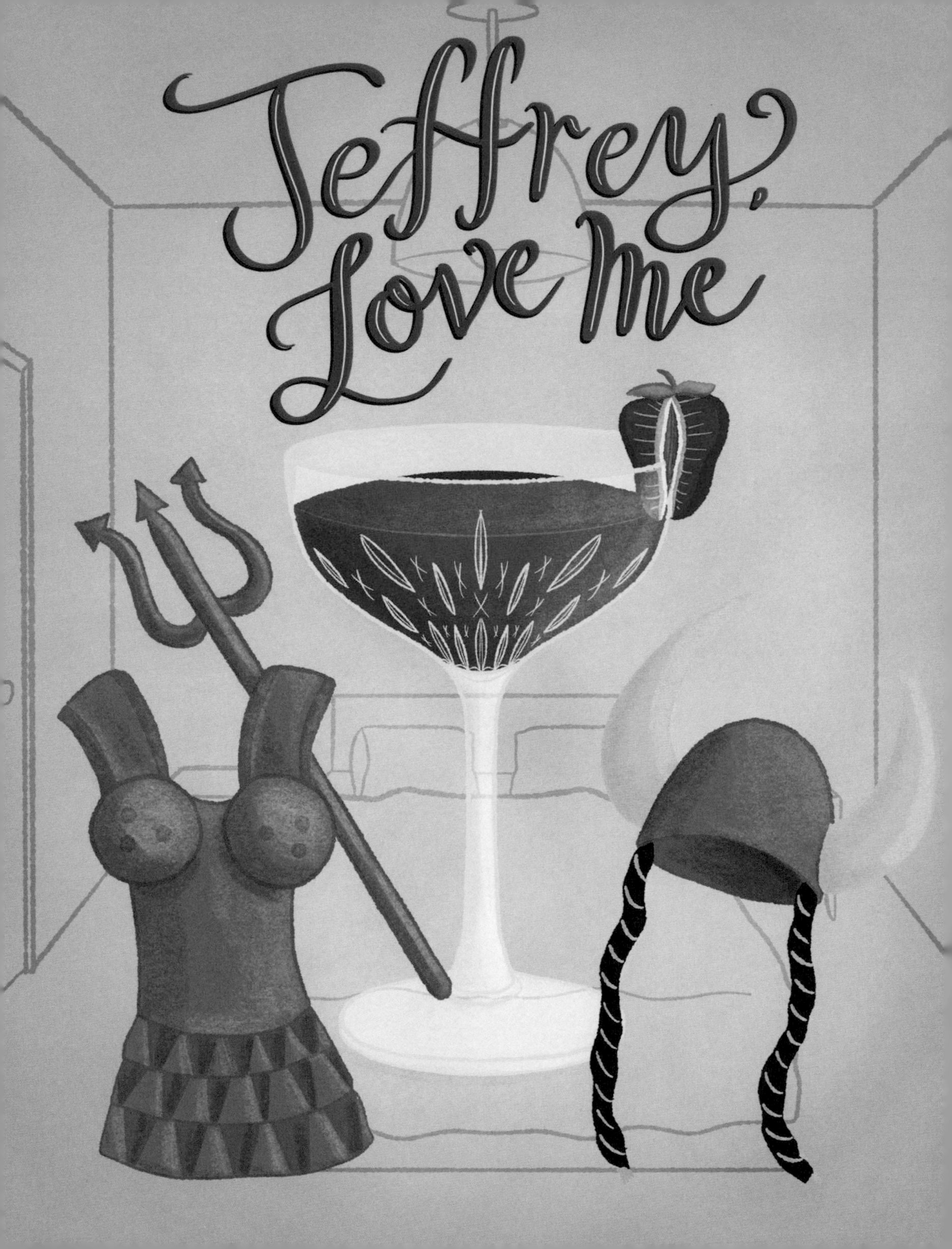
Jeffrey, Love Me

# JEFFREY, LOVE ME

Strawberries appear right after chocolate on the list of top aphrodisiacs. The love connection goes all the way back to Roman times, when the berries were a symbol of Venus. Strawberries were a symbol of fertility because of their visible exterior seeds. Whether you shake or blend this frosé, it's sure to get you as frisky as Maude Lebowski hunting for a baby daddy.

## INGREDIENTS

1½ ounces blanco tequila

1 ounce rosé wine

1 ounce strawberry puree
(recipe page 41)

½ ounce simple syrup
(recipe page 58)

1 fresh strawberry, for garnish

## DIRECTIONS

Using a shaker, shake the tequila, wine, strawberry puree, and simple syrup with ice.

Strain into a cocktail glass and garnish with a strawberry.

*Song Pairing*
## "LOOKIN' OUT MY BACK DOOR"
by Creedence Clearwater Revival

# REASONABLE ALLOWANCE

What a surprise. The supposedly self-made millionaire Jeffrey Lebowski is a fraud. In fact, he may be in on Bunny's kidnapping so he could pull a million dollars out of his ex-wife's foundation's account—with no intent to pay the ransom. As the Dude and Walter discover, there was likely no ransom money in the bag. The Big Lebowski's story begins to unravel when Maude reveals that she provides her father with a reasonable allowance. Toast to the fake rich everywhere with this twist on the classic Millionaire, a Prohibition-era cocktail that is all (actual) luxury.

## INGREDIENTS

2 ounces rye whiskey

¾ ounce Grand Marnier

¼ ounce grenadine

¼ ounce fresh lemon juice

2 dashes absinthe or Pernod

1 egg white (see page 22)

## DIRECTIONS

Add the rye, Grand Marnier, grenadine, lemon juice, absinthe, and egg white to a shaker with ice.

Shake vigorously and strain into a cocktail glass.

*Song Pairing*
"STAMPING GROUND"
by Moondog

REASONABLE ALLOWANCE

# STRANGER IN THE ALPS

"Larry, see what happens when you find a stranger in the Alps?!"
This edited-for-TV version of Walter Sobchak's infamous line,
delivered repeatedly while Walter beats Larry's neighbor's car with a
bat, became a huge internet sensation. It even inspired the title of
a critically acclaimed Phoebe Bridgers album. Génépy des Alpes is a
delightful alpine liqueur hailing from France and is widely available
in liquor stores and online. This cocktail is what happens when you
find a stranger in the Alps!

## INGREDIENTS

1½ ounces gin

½ ounce Génépy des Alpes

2 ounces fresh lemon juice

¼ ounce simple syrup (recipe page 58)

2 dashes orange bitters

Lemon twist, for garnish

## DIRECTIONS

Using a shaker, shake the gin, Génépy,
lemon juice, simple syrup, and bitters
with ice.

Strain into a chilled cocktail glass.

Garnish with a lemon twist.

*Album Pairing*

**STRANGER IN THE ALPS**
by Phoebe Bridgers

# STAY OUT OF MALIBU

The Malibu police chief does not like your jerk-off name or your jerk-off face or your jerk-off behavior. So why don't you just stay out of Malibu? Because it's so damned delicious, that's why. Especially when combined with mango juice and a dose of sparkling wine. This coconut rum number is so good, you'll never stay out of Malibu. But watch out for that hangover if you consume too many!

## INGREDIENTS

1½ ounces coconut rum, such as Malibu

¾ ounce canned mango juice

¾ ounce fresh lime juice

2 ounces sparkling wine

## DIRECTIONS

Using a shaker, shake the rum, mango juice, and lime juice with ice.

Pour into a rocks glass with a large ice cube.

Top with the sparkling wine.

Song Pairing
"BRANDED (THEME SONG)"
by Kitsch and Camp

# Stay Out Of Malibu

# CHINSTRAP

# CHINSTRAP

The chinstrap beard, a line of facial hair following the jawline, came into fashion in the late 1700s and continued through the nineteenth century. Today, it is sometimes still seen on men trying to define their chin or cover a weight problem—we presume Walter Sobchak's reason for the style is a little bit of both. Plus, he surely feels it adds a touch of masculinity and panache befitting a combat veteran.

## INGREDIENTS

Kosher salt, for garnish

1 ounce bourbon whiskey

1 ounce applejack

¾ ounce fresh lime juice

½ ounce simple syrup (recipe page 58)

## DIRECTIONS

Salt the rim of a rocks glass (see page 18).

Using a shaker, shake the whiskey, applejack, lime juice, and simple syrup with ice.

Pour into the prepared glass.

# TREEHORN

Porn producer and loan shark Jackie Treehorn throws one heck of a garden party. There's dancing, fire sticks, and naked people on trampolines (in slow motion!). This is Malibu, after all, where sleaze has an artistic sheen. The party soundtrack is famed Peruvian singer Yma Sumac, who garnered international fame in the 1950s with her astounding five-octave vocal range. The most Peruvian of cocktails, the pisco sour, is the inspiration here.

## INGREDIENTS

1½ ounces pisco

¾ ounce Grand Marnier

¾ ounce fresh lemon or lime juice

2 dashes orange bitters

## DIRECTIONS

Using a shaker, shake the pisco, Grand Marnier, lemon juice, and bitters with ice.

Strain into a cocktail glass.

*Song Pairing*

"ATAYPURA!"
by Yma Sumac

*Dude Fact*

Jackie Treehorn's house is named the Sheats-Goldstein Residence and has appeared in a number of movies and TV shows, including Snowfall, Southland, and Bandits.

Modestly Priced Receptacle

# MODESTLY PRICED RECEPTACLE

Everyone knows that the final scam by The Man is death. Even if you don't want a fancy box and a hillside dotted with fresh-cut flowers, you're gonna pay. But how can funeral homes still fleece you when the choice is cremation? The urn. Donny's ashes have to go somewhere, and it's a $180 fancy bucket (more than $300, adjusted for inflation). What's wrong with just putting the remains in a spent Folgers coffee can from a nearby Ralph's supermarket? Bingo, that's exactly what Walter and the Dude want to know.

## INGREDIENTS

1½ ounces aged rum

¾ ounce coffee liqueur

¼ ounce allspice dram

2 ounces fresh pineapple juice

## DIRECTIONS

Using a shaker, shake the rum, coffee liqueur, allspice dram, and pineapple juice with ice.

Pour into a rocks glass.

# PORT HURON STATEMENT

Running through his extensive curriculum vitae while in bed post-coitus with Maude Lebowski, the Dude reveals he played a part in drafting the Port Huron Statement (he clarifies: the first one, not the one that made compromises). The very real 1962 political manifesto written by student activists is named after the town in which it was conceived, Port Huron, Michigan. Join the students—and a younger Dude—in toasting to a more just, more egalitarian, and less racist country with a Michigan mead-based cocktail. Mead, made from fermented honey, is an ancient beverage that works wonders in mixed drinks.

## INGREDIENTS

1½ ounces applejack

1½ ounces gold mead

½ ounce fresh lemon juice

Lemon peel, for garnish

## DIRECTIONS

Using a shaker, shake the applejack, mead, and lemon juice with ice.

Strain into a cocktail glass.

Garnish with a lemon peel.

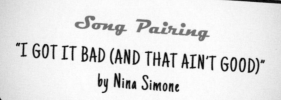

*Song Pairing*
"I GOT IT BAD (AND THAT AIN'T GOOD)"
by Nina Simone

# PORT HURON STATEMENT

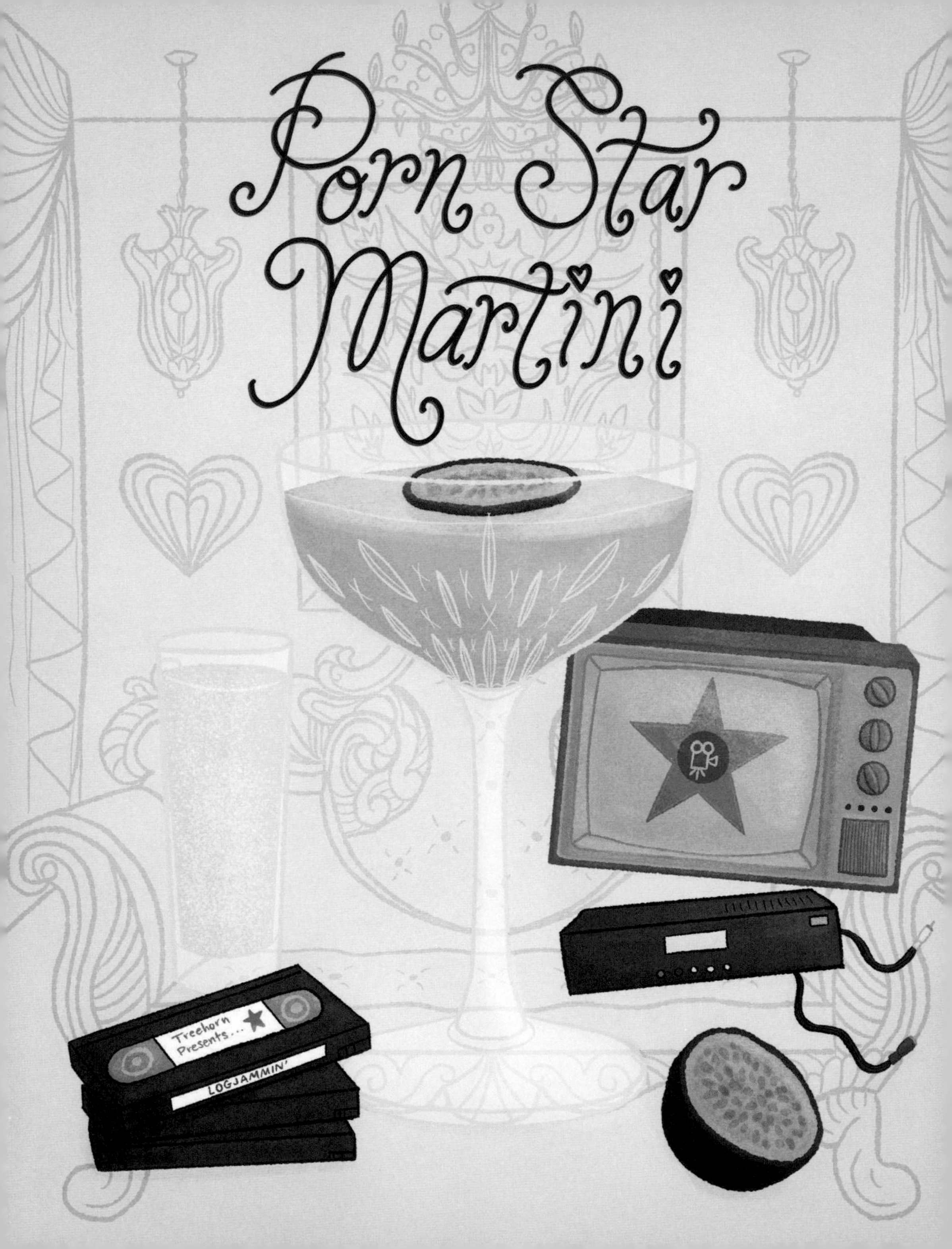
Porn Star Martini
Treehorn Presents...
LOGJAMMIN'

# PORN STAR MARTINI

It's well known that Bunny Lebowski made at least one adult movie (*Logjammin'*) for Jackie Treehorn. According to stepdaughter Maude Lebowski, it all came to pass because Bunny is a nymphomaniac incapable of love. Luckily, there's a cocktail for such individuals, created by a fella by the name of Douglas Ankrah, which combines the strong flavors of vanilla and passion fruit for a true global classic.

## VANILLA SIMPLE SYRUP

½ cup water

½ cup sugar

1 teaspoon vanilla extract

## COCKTAIL

1½ ounces vanilla vodka

½ ounce passion fruit liqueur

1 ounce canned passion fruit puree

½ ounce fresh lime juice

½ ounce Vanilla Simple Syrup

½ fresh passion fruit, for garnish

2 ounces chilled sparkling wine

## DIRECTIONS

To make the vanilla simple syrup: Bring the water to a boil, then remove from the heat.

Add the sugar and stir to dissolve. Add the vanilla and let the mixture steep for 30 minutes.

Store in the refrigerator in an airtight container for up to 2 weeks.

To make the cocktail: Using a shaker, shake the vodka, passion fruit liqueur, passion fruit puree, lime juice, and simple syrup with ice.

Strain into a cocktail glass.

Garnish with the passion fruit. Serve with sparkling wine on the side in a shot glass.

*Song Pairing*

"LUJON"

by Henry Mancini

# HUMAN PARAQUAT

Paraquat is a widely used herbicide that is available in the US but has been banned in the European Union since 2007. It has been linked to degenerative disorders such as Parkinson's disease. In the 1970s, the US government sprayed paraquat on cannabis fields in Mexico, which is how it came to the attention of the Dude. The Big Lebowski is indeed a human paraquat. A delightful, drinkable version can be made with (nonsprayed) crushed mint.

## INGREDIENTS

2½ ounces reposado tequila

1 ounce fresh lime juice

1 ounce simple syrup (recipe page 58)

2 dashes orange bitters

10 to 12 fresh mint leaves

## DIRECTIONS

Using a shaker, shake the tequila, lime juice, simple syrup, bitters, and mint leaves with ice.

Pour into a rocks glass.

# Human Paraquat

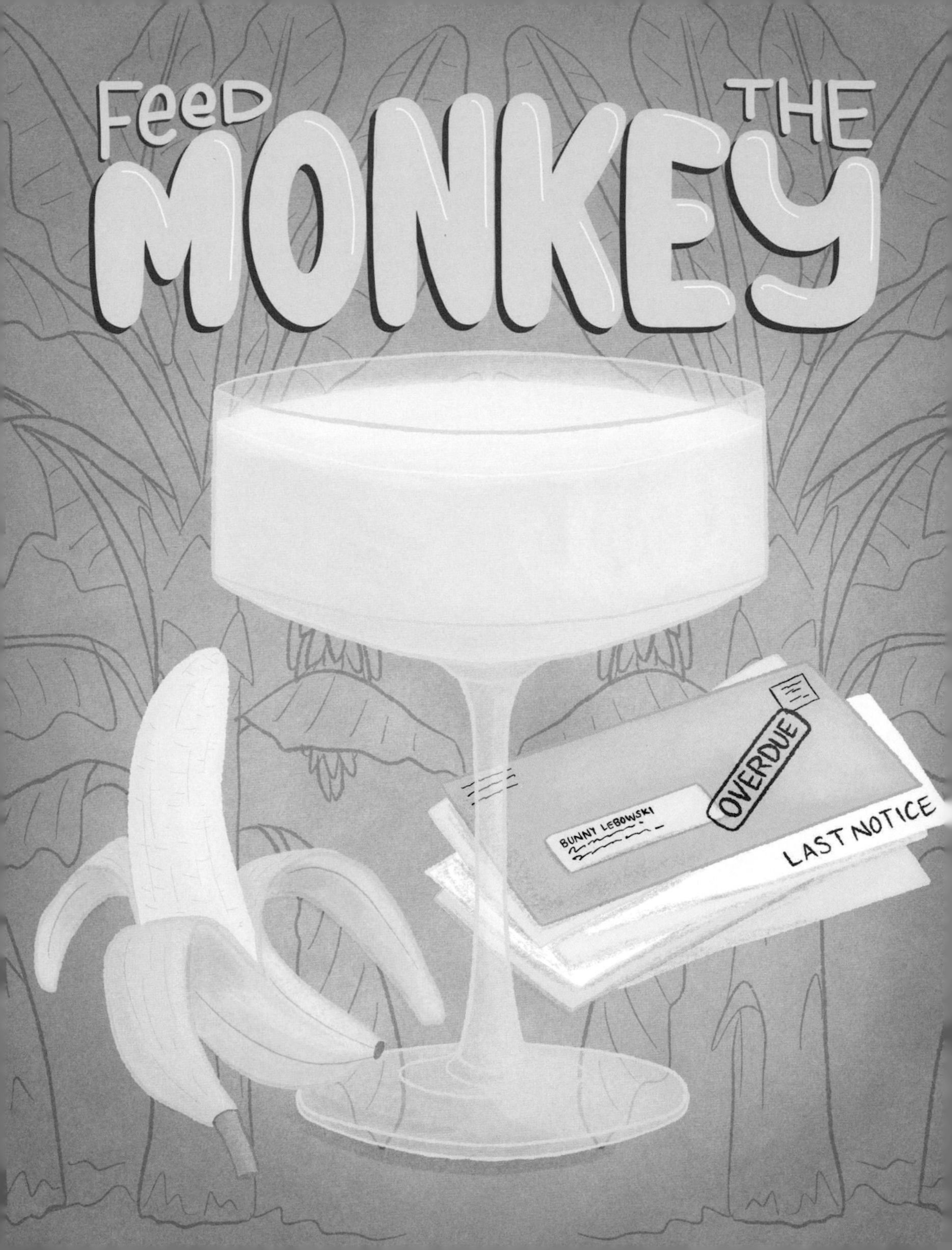
Feed THE MONKEY
OVERDUE
BUNNY LEBOWSKI
LAST NOTICE

# FEED THE MONKEY

Why did Bunny Lebowski fake her own kidnapping? Because she owes money all over town, including to known pornographers. And because, according to the Dude, she is a nympho who needs to "feed the monkey." The Dude is referring to feeding her, er, addiction. Feed your addiction to the intoxicating blend of juniper, banana, and vanilla with this knockout nip.

### INGREDIENTS

1½ ounces gin

½ ounce Galliano

¾ ounce banana liqueur

½ ounce cream

### DIRECTIONS

Using a shaker, shake the gin, Galliano, banana liqueur, and cream with ice.

Strain into a cocktail glass.

*Song Pairing*

"MY MOOD SWINGS"
by Elvis Costello

# STAR LANES

Bowling peaked in the United States in the mid-1960s, when there were a total of around twelve thousand alleys. Hollywood Star Lanes on Santa Monica Boulevard opened in 1960 and closed in 2002. It featured thirty-two lanes and, importantly for the Coen Brothers, manual scoring (see page 54). The interior of the neon-lit alley appears many times in *The Big Lebowski*, and so do the stars on the exterior of the building—which are retro and far-out. They appear whenever the trio of the Dude, Walter, and Donny leave the bowling alley, but also when the Dude follows Maude on her magic carpet in his dreams.

## INGREDIENTS

2 ounces gin

¾ ounce fresh lemon juice

½ ounce sarsaparilla syrup

2 ounces club soda

Lemon peel, for garnish

## DIRECTIONS

Using a shaker, shake the gin, lemon juice, and sarsaparilla syrup with ice.

Strain into a rocks glass filled with ice.

Top with the club soda and garnish with a lemon peel.

# DONNY'S ASHES

Donny loved the outdoors. He was a good bowler. He loved the Pacific and explored California beaches surfing—from La Jolla to Leo Carrillo, and even to Pismo. Like so many men of his generation, he died before his time. Raise a glass to Donny. Note: To make this drink in honor of Theodore Donald Kerabatsos for a crowd, simply convert ounces in the recipe below to cups (see page 18).

## INGREDIENTS

Black salt, for garnish

1½ ounces ouzo

2 ounces fresh pineapple juice

½ ounce fresh lime juice

## DIRECTIONS

Rim a rocks glass with the black salt (see page 15).

Using a shaker, shake the ouzo, pineapple juice, and lime juice with ice.

Pour into the prepared glass.

*Dude Fact*

It's part of Coen Brothers movie lore that the bodies of Steve Buscemi's characters end up in successively worse shape in each movie: as a corpse in Miller's Crossing, a leg in Fargo, and ashes in The Big Lebowski.

*Song Pairing*

"DEAD FLOWERS" by Townes Van Zandt

*Cocktails that do not contain citrus, dairy, or eggs* are stirred together in a mixing glass. Because they are not as diluted by juices as shaken drinks, they are typically higher in ABV (alcohol by volume) and are referred to as spiritous or spirit-forward cocktails. Think martinis, sidecars, Negronis, and more. In this chapter you will find Maude's preferred Manhattan as well as the favorite Nordic drink of the Knutsons, Bunny's family from Moorhead, Minnesota.

# BUNNY TOE

When the Dude first meets Bunny Lebowski, she is sitting poolside and painting her toes green. Later, after the Dude and Walter fail to deliver the ransom money, the Nihilists send a severed green toe to the Big Lebowski. Since Bunny was never kidnapped, whose toe is it?! Turns out, the digit belonged to a girlfriend of a Nihilist—she thought they were getting a million dollars. You want a toe? There are ways to get you a toe.

## INGREDIENTS

1 ounce London Dry gin

1 ounce Midori

1 ounce dry vermouth

2 dashes orange bitters

Cocktail cherry, for garnish

## DIRECTIONS

Add the gin, Midori, dry vermouth, and bitters to a mixing glass with ice.

Stir and strain into a cocktail glass.

Garnish with a cocktail cherry.

# THE NIHILIST

The Nihilists are led by Uli Kunkel (a.k.a. porn star Karl Hungus). They include Franz and Dieter and their girlfriends. They have a plan to defraud the Big Lebowski of a million dollars by pretending they have kidnapped Bunny. Originally, the group was also part of the band Autobahn, who released an album entitled *Nagelbett* (see page 117). But what are nihilists? Well, they believe in nothing. Must be exhausting.

## INGREDIENTS

2 ounces rye whiskey

¼ ounce Goldschläger

2 dashes Angostura bitters

Orange peel, for garnish

## DIRECTIONS

Add the rye, Goldschläger, and bitters to a mixing glass with ice.

Stir and strain into a rocks glass with a large ice cube.

Garnish with an orange peel.

*Song Pairing*
"WIE GLAUBEN"
by Carter Burwell

*Dude Fact*
One of the Nihilists is played by Flea from the band Red Hot Chili Peppers.

# ROLL ON SATURDAY

Do not ask Walter Sobchak to bowl on Saturday. Saturday is the Shabbos (sabbath) for this Polish Catholic turned Jew. He does not work, he does not drive a car, he does not ride in a car, he does not handle money, and he does not even turn on the oven. He also does not drink on Saturday—except for health purposes (he also can't use a phone unless it's an emergency). But Jägermeister with its many herbs is good for coughs and sore throats. A perfect Shabbos drink.

### INGREDIENTS

2 ounces vodka

½ ounce plum brandy

½ ounce Jägermeister

2 dashes orange bitters

### DIRECTIONS

Add the vodka, brandy, Jägermeister, and bitters to a mixing glass with ice.

Stir and strain into a rocks glass with a large ice cube.

# ROLL ON SATURDAY

TODAY IS
SATURDAY

Maude's Manhattan

# MAUDE'S MANHATTAN

Maude Lebowski is a feminist avant-garde artist. Her work has been commended for being strong . . . vaginally. But Maude is also a woman with serious business brains, which she inherited from her mother. She knows what she wants, and this includes coitus in order to conceive a child—preferably with a man she does not have to see again socially. The Dude will do, and she soon becomes his f\*\*king lady friend.

## INGREDIENTS

2 ounces brandy

½ ounce amaro, such as Averna

½ ounce Chambord

2 dashes orange bitters

Fresh raspberry, for garnish

## DIRECTIONS

Add the brandy, amaro, Chambord, and orange bittersr to a mixing glass with ice.

Stir and strain into a cocktail glass.

Garnish with a raspberry.

Song Pairing

"WALKING SONG"
by Meredith Monk

# TENDER RESIGNATION

The Dude believes he must tender his resignation, or whatever, after he sees proof of Bunny's kidnapping in the form of a severed toe. The Dude thinks his detective work has been faulty. Maude, however, doesn't buy it. Why? Because you don't kidnap someone you're acquainted with. The kidnapper, Uli, was in a porn film with Bunny called *Logjammin'*—so they know each other. This new information offers a lot of strands to keep in old Duder's head.

## INGREDIENTS

1½ ounces vodka

¾ ounce Campari

¾ ounce Kahlúa

Orange peel, for garnish

## DIRECTIONS

Add the vodka, Campari, and Kahlúa to a mixing glass with ice.

Stir and strain into a rocks glass with a large ice cube.

Garnish with an orange peel.

# TENDER RESIGNATION

# FERRET IN THE BATHTUB
## (Nice Marmot)

# FERRET IN THE BATHTUB
## (NICE MARMOT)

The Dude is relaxing in the tub when he is rudely interrupted by the Nihilists. Uli and his friends have brought a marmot (a ferret) with which to instill a special kind of fear. And it works, because they toss the aggressive fur ball into the tub between the legs of a very naked Dude. Rude. It's the equivalent of tossing a minty digestif into a White Russian. Wrong (but so right)!

## INGREDIENTS

1½ ounces vodka

1 ounce Kahlúa

½ ounce cream

1 ounce Fernet-Branca

## DIRECTIONS

Add the vodka, Kahlúa, and cream to a mixing glass with ice.

Stir and strain into a rocks glass.

Pour the Fernet into a shot glass and serve it on the side or lower it into the cocktail. Whichever way you like it, make sure to consume them together.

# ZESTY ENTERPRISE

Maude Lebowski considers sex, or coitus, a "zesty enterprise." The other zesty enterprise is, of course, cocktailing—and this mixed drink employs extra citrus zest. It is inspired by a famed number called the Flame of Love (made for crooner Dean Martin, who is featured in the film's soundtrack). The trick to it is simple: light the oil in the orange peel over the drink, not yourself.

## INGREDIENTS

2½ ounces gin

½ ounce Cointreau

2 dashes orange bitters

3 orange peels

## DIRECTIONS

Add the gin, Cointreau, and bitters to a mixing glass with ice.

Stir and strain into a cocktail glass.

Using a lighter, flick open the flame using one hand while your other hand squeezes an orange peel so that the oils squirt out and through the flame and into the glass.

Rim the glass with the orange peel and remaining oils and discard. Repeat with the remaining 2 orange peels.

🔥 **FIRE-SAFETY NOTES**

- Make sure you're sober when using fire.
- Always make sure your hands, the counter, the lighter, and anything else you don't want to set on fire have no alcohol on them. In fact, it's best to remove anything flammable from your prep area.
- Do not use a plastic cup or a plastic straw near fire.
- Sometimes fire is hard to see, especially if you're in an area with a lot of light, so try turning down the lights so you can see the flame, but not so much that you can't see what you're doing.

*Song Pairing*
**"STANDING ON THE CORNER"**
*by Dean Martin*

# NAGELBETT (BED OF NAILS)

*Nagelbett* is an LP by the band Autobahn, and Maude has a copy of the record at her house. The techno-pop album features such riveting classics as "Take It In" and "Edelweiss (Club Mix)." Uli Kunkel was the lead singer of this band, and its former members are now Nihilists demanding ransom money from the Dude. The venerable rusty nail cocktail features Scotch and the spiced liqueur Drambuie. How much stronger is a whole bed of nails? Find out with the addition of Benedictine, another herbaceous liqueur, which contains twenty-seven unique herbs and spices. Just enough flavor-nails to lie on comfortably.

## INGREDIENTS

1¼ ounces Scotch whisky

¾ ounce Drambuie

¼ ounce Benedictine

Orange peel, for garnish

## DIRECTIONS

Add the Scotch, Drambuie, and Benedictine to a rocks glass with ice.

Stir and garnish with an orange peel.

# THE KNUTSONS

Who the f**k are the Knutsons? It's a good question. The Knutsons are Bunny Lebowski's parents (we learn she is a runaway named Fawn Knutson). They will not be too pleased when they find out their daughter has been in pornographic movies with Karl Hungus. Private detective Da Fino has been sent to find her, paid for by this loving (and worried) family from Moorhead, Minnesota.

## INGREDIENTS

2 ounces aquavit

1 ounce dry vermouth

Cocktail onion, for garnish

## DIRECTIONS

Add the aquavit and dry vermouth to a mixing glass with ice.

Stir and strain into a cocktail glass.

Garnish with a cocktail onion.

Song Pairing

"TAMMY"
by Debbie Reynolds

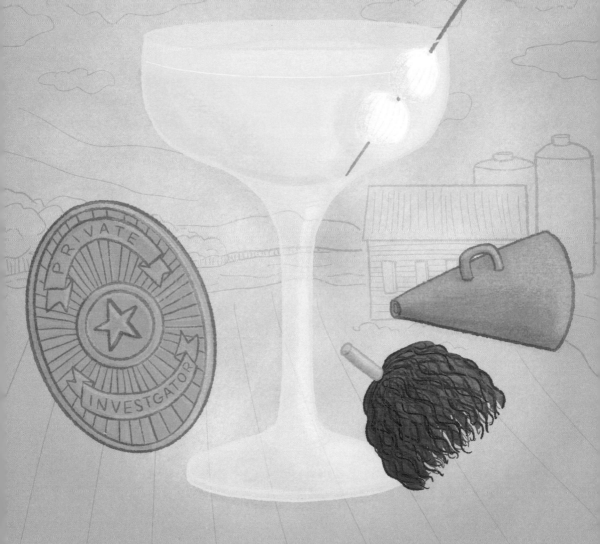

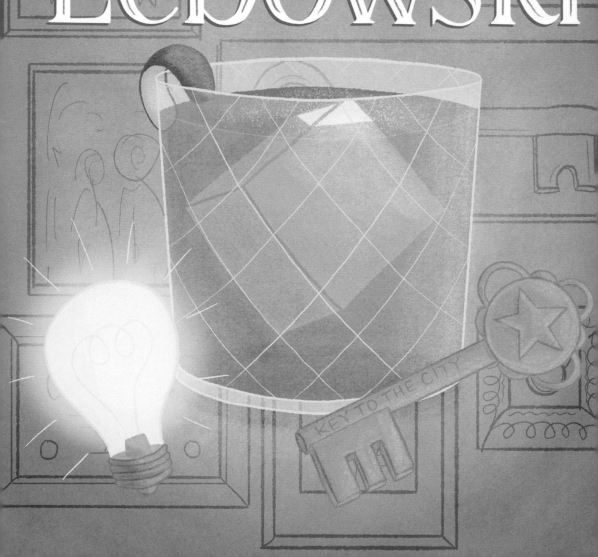

# The BIG Lebowski

# THE BIG LEBOWSKI

As the Big Lebowski tells it, he is a self-made man who has accomplished more than most—and without the use of his legs. Of course, none of his story is true; he's an embezzler who lives on a reasonable allowance (see page 76). But appearances must be kept up. In fact, appearances are all there is. The Big Lebowski drinks expensive liquor. His favorite drink is an old-fashioned, made with the priciest cognac you can get your greedy little hands on.

### INGREDIENTS

2 ounces cognac

¼ ounce Grand Marnier

Dash Angostura bitters

Dash orange bitters

Orange peel, for garnish

### DIRECTIONS

Add the cognac, Grand Marnier, and bitters to a shaker with ice.

Stir and strain into a rocks glass with a large ice cube.

Express (see page 18) an orange peel over the top of the drink and discard.

### Song Pairing

MOZART'S REQUIEM IN D MINOR, K.626: I. "INTROITUS"
by Nikolaus Harnoncourt, Vienna State Opera Chorus

### Dude Fact

Before the Coen Brothers settled on David Huddleston to play the character Big Lebowski, they considered Marlon Brando, Gene Hackman, Robert Duvall, and Anthony Hopkins.

# MOONLESS PRAIRIE NIGHT

When the Dude is drugged by Jackie Treehorn, darkness washes over him. As the cowboy Stranger (Sam Elliott) narrator explains, this darkness is darker than a black steer's tuchus on a moonless prairie night. Now that is dark. This cocktail happens to be 1) real dark and 2) delicious with steer, or a good steak. In fact, this may be your new go-to with all things beef.

## INGREDIENTS

2 ounces bourbon whiskey

1 ounce amaro, such as Averna

¼ ounce Angostura bitters

Orange peel, for garnish

## DIRECTIONS

Add the whiskey, amaro, and bitters to a mixing glass with ice.

Stir and strain into a cocktail glass.

Garnish with an orange peel.

# BUMS ALWAYS LOSE

## *Serves 6 to 8*

According to the Big Lebowski, bums always lose. But the irony is that the Big L is just as much of a bum as the Dude; his wife was the one with the money, and he lives on a reasonable allowance (see page 76). What's more, this proclaimed self-made man is terrible at business. He really is a human paraquat (see page 92). Bums, of course, love wine, and this punch is perfect for serving a group of losers who lose.

## INGREDIENTS

2 bottles (750 ml each) red table wine

1 cup brandy

½ cup triple sec

1 cup fresh orange juice

1 cup pomegranate juice

½ cup simple syrup, or more to taste (recipe page 58)

Fresh orange slices, for garnish

Fresh apple slices, for garnish

Fresh blackberries, for garnish

Fresh pomegranate seeds, for garnish

## DIRECTIONS

In a large punch bowl with ice, combine the wine, brandy, triple sec, orange juice, pomegranate juice, and simple syrup.

Stir until thoroughly combined.

Garnish with orange slices, apple slices, blackberries, and pomegranate seeds.

# STRIKES AND GUTTERS

Life is full of ups and downs, strikes and gutters. As the Dude says, you can't be worrying so much about s**t. Life goes on. Don't get too down about things, because you never know when the next strike is going to hit. A great way to take it easy is with this relaxed, bowling-friendly version of a margarita. The beer softens the drink into an effortless sipper.

## INGREDIENTS

2 ounces reposado tequila

¼ ounce simple syrup (recipe page 58)

2 dashes orange bitters

2 ounces beer, preferably Mexican lager

## DIRECTIONS

Add the tequila, simple syrup, and bitters to a shaker.

Stir and strain into a rocks glass with a large ice cube.

Top with the beer.

*Song Pairing*

"BEHAVE YOURSELF"
by Booker T. and
the M.G.'s

# WHALE SONG

Put on your headphones, cue the serene music, and slide into this warm cocktail for a true spa experience. Follow the Dude's lead and relax to the sounds of bowling tournaments or whale songs, whatever works for you. This black tea toddy is the perfect accompaniment to winding down. Feel free to double or quadruple this recipe for a group meditation session. Or, add a little cream, as the Dude surely would, for an extra-soothing libation.

## INGREDIENTS

6 ounces brewed hot black tea

1½ ounces rum

1 ounce heavy cream (optional)

Nutmeg, for garnish

## DIRECTIONS

To your mug of hot tea, stir in the rum and cream, if using.

Grind fresh nutmeg over the top of the beverage.

### Song Pairing

The ambient noise of whale sounds or bowling tournaments.

# THE
# BOOK OF
# White
# Russians

*Whether you are at a bowling alley, in a limousine,* or doing yoga in your living room, a White Russian is the perfect companion. The drink we know as the White Russian likely got its start in the 1960s, a riff on the Black Russian with the addition of cream. And who came up with the Black Russian? The story goes that a barman named Gustav Tops invented the cocktail at the Hotel Metropole in Brussels in 1949. The drink isn't Russian at all, just named so because it features vodka. Whence the cream? While hard to imagine now, cream drinks were all the rage in the 1960s, from grasshoppers to pink squirrels. The Black Russian got dosed by association, like a cream contact high. This section includes the classic recipe as well as important variations. For the industrious, there is even a clarified White Russian punch, a showstopping mix perfect for a party (or resting in the fridge to enjoy over time).

# THE DUDE (WHITE RUSSIAN)

For most of us, the White Russian, with its notes of vanilla, caramel, and coffee, is most appropriate as a digestif after a meal or as a fireside sipper. Not so for the Dude. Jeffrey Lebowski drinks a White Russian, which he also calls a Caucasian, throughout the day and night. He consumes them at home in the tub, at the bowling alley, in a moving limousine, while practicing Tai Chi, at Jackie Treehorn's house, and at Maude's loft (notably, with powdered creamer). It's inspiring, really, to see one man's devotion to a single drink. In an interview, Jeff Dowd, the real-life inspiration for the Dude, says of the choice: "The reason it was White Russians is you could have a lot more fun with a White Russian than you can with, say, a vodka soda." True enough.

## INGREDIENTS

2 ounces vodka

1 ounce Kahlúa

Splash heavy cream

## DIRECTIONS

Combine the vodka, Kahlúa, and heavy cream in a rocks glass over ice.

*Dude Fact*

Characters in *The Big Lebowski* say "dude" 161 times in the film.

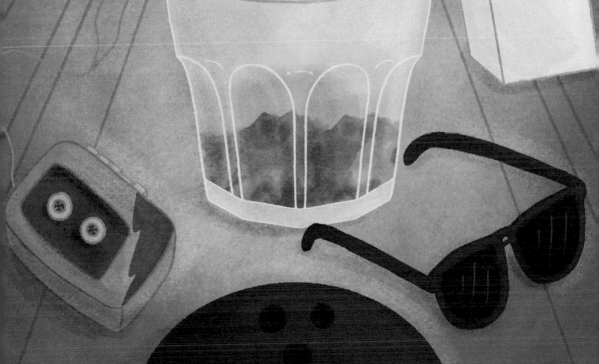

# the DUDE
## (White Russian)

# HIS DUDENESS

There are a few variations of the White Russian cocktail. It can be shaken instead of built in the glass, for instance, or even warmed. But to really unlock the drink's full potential, it should be made with espresso (or strong coffee) and receive an extra dose of flavor from amaro. Think of this as the elevated take, a version appropriate for special celebrations (or anytime). Creating the drink from the ground up, perfect piece by perfect piece, really ties the drink together. You will taste the difference and may never go back.

## INGREDIENTS

1 ounce vodka

½ ounce aged rum

½ ounce amaro, such as Averna

1 ounce freshly brewed espresso or strong-brewed coffee

1 ounce heavy cream

½ ounce simple syrup (recipe page 58)

## DIRECTIONS

Combine the vodka, rum, amaro, espresso, cream, and simple syrup in a rocks glass with ice.

Stir and enjoy.

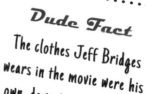

*Dude Fact*

The clothes Jeff Bridges wears in the movie were his own, down to the T-shirts and jelly slippers.

# EL DUDERINO

Replacing the heavy cream in a White Russian with horchata, a traditional Mexican drink made with white rice, makes for great texture and novel flavor. It is a perfect substitute during hot weather or at outdoor fêtes. Lose the robe, slip on sunglasses, and enjoy this deliciously smooth concoction. Our film is set in Southern California—so of course the Dude refers to himself as El Duderino.

## INGREDIENTS

2 ounces vodka

1 ounce Kahlúa

3 ounces horchata

Ground cinnamon, for garnish

## DIRECTION

Using a shaker, shake the vodka, Kahlúa, and horchata with ice.

Pour into a rocks glass.

Garnish with cinnamon.

*Song Pairing*
"OYE COMO VA"
by Santana

*Dude Fact*
The Dude drinks nine White Russians in the movie.

# YOUNG JEFFREY

## *Serves 5*

We can only imagine what the Dude was like when he was younger. We suspect that, at one time, he could have been—dare we say it?—ambitious. He may have even held a job before he became the pot-smoking, bowling slacker that we know and love. Channel an industrious Dude with this clarified milk punch. Although it takes a bit of work in assembly, it can be enjoyed lazily for days after. You will love the texture.

### INGREDIENTS

8 ounces whole milk

2 ounces fresh lemon juice

1 cup hot, freshly brewed coffee

8 ounces vodka

⅛ cup sugar

5 ounces dark rum

### DIRECTIONS

In a medium saucepan over medium-high heat, bring the milk to a boil, then immediately remove the pan from the heat.

Stir in the lemon juice and let the mixture sit for 5 minutes.

In a medium bowl, combine the hot coffee, vodka, sugar, and rum and stir until the sugar dissolves.

Pour the coffee mixture slowly into the milk while stirring to combine thoroughly.

Pour the resulting mixture through a cheesecloth and then strain again through a second cheesecloth.

Finally, strain the mixture using a coffee filter into a sealable bottle or jar and refrigerate at least an hour to cool.

Add to your cocktail glass of choice and serve.

### Dude Fact

In the first draft of the script, the Dude was the heir to the Rubik's Cube fortune.

# RUSSIAN PUMPKIN

Let's say, for argument's sake, that the Dude is making one of his visitations and only pumpkin spice creamer is available. Since we know his Dudeness does not hesitate to use powdered creamer, we can safely assume he would not let a little pumpkin spice get in the way of a drink either. As luck would have it, this is a delicious addition that is ideal on an extra-chilly morning or around the holidays. In the recipe that follows, use either pumpkin spice creamer or dry pumpkin pie spice.

## INGREDIENTS

2 ounces vodka

1 ounce Kahlúa

Splash heavy cream

Dash pumpkin pie spice or splash pumpkin spice creamer

## DIRECTION

Using a shaker, shake the vodka, Kahlúa, heavy cream, and pumpkin pie spice with ice.

Pour into a rocks glass.

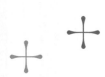

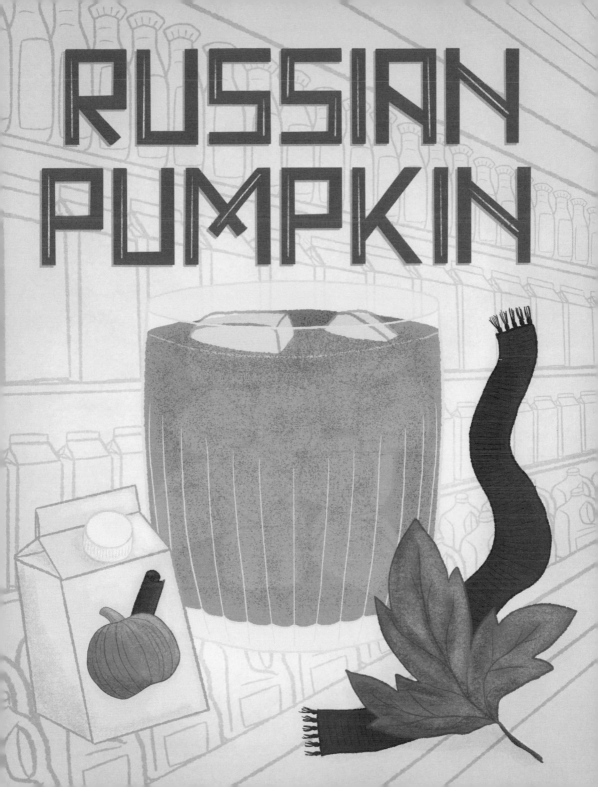

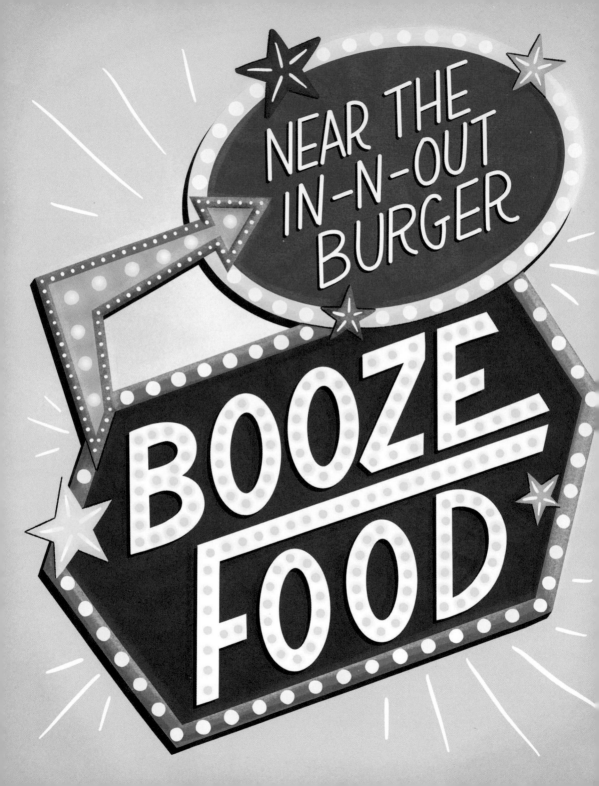

***THE BIG LEBOWSKI** features a few iconic food scenes.*

We see wrappers from the famed Los Angeles In-N-Out Burger chain on the Dude's coffee table—so we already know that excursions there are part of his life. When Walter discovers the address of alleged car thief Larry Sellers, Donny is excited that an In-N-Out Burger is nearby. Following the visit to Larry's house, we see the Dude, Walter, and Donny enjoying the aftermath of an In-N-Out stop. In proper Los Angeles style, the Nihilists visit a diner and order food: notably lingonberry pancakes and pigs in a blanket. In addition to these items, in this chapter you'll find recipes for bowling alley popcorn as well as a couple of desserts. All are great accompaniments to a *Big Lebowski* movie-watching party or cocktail session.

# STAR LANES POPCORN

## *Serves 4*

Channel the Star Lanes bowling alley, where the Dude and his team hang out, with this delightfully zesty snack. The taste is pure Southern Californian Americana. Mixed drinks based on tequila or whiskey are the ideal foil here.

## INGREDIENTS

⅓ cup (65 g) popcorn kernels

3 tablespoons vegetable oil

2 teaspoons taco seasoning, such as Old El Paso

Fresh lime zest, for garnish

## DIRECTIONS

Stir together the popcorn and oil in a small bowl.

Heat a medium Dutch oven or saucepan over medium-high heat.

Add the popcorn and oil mixture and cover. Cook 2 to 3 minutes, until the popcorn stops popping.

Remove the popcorn from the heat and transfer to a paper bag or bowl.

Add the taco seasoning and toss until the popcorn is coated.

Serve in bowls topped with lime zest.

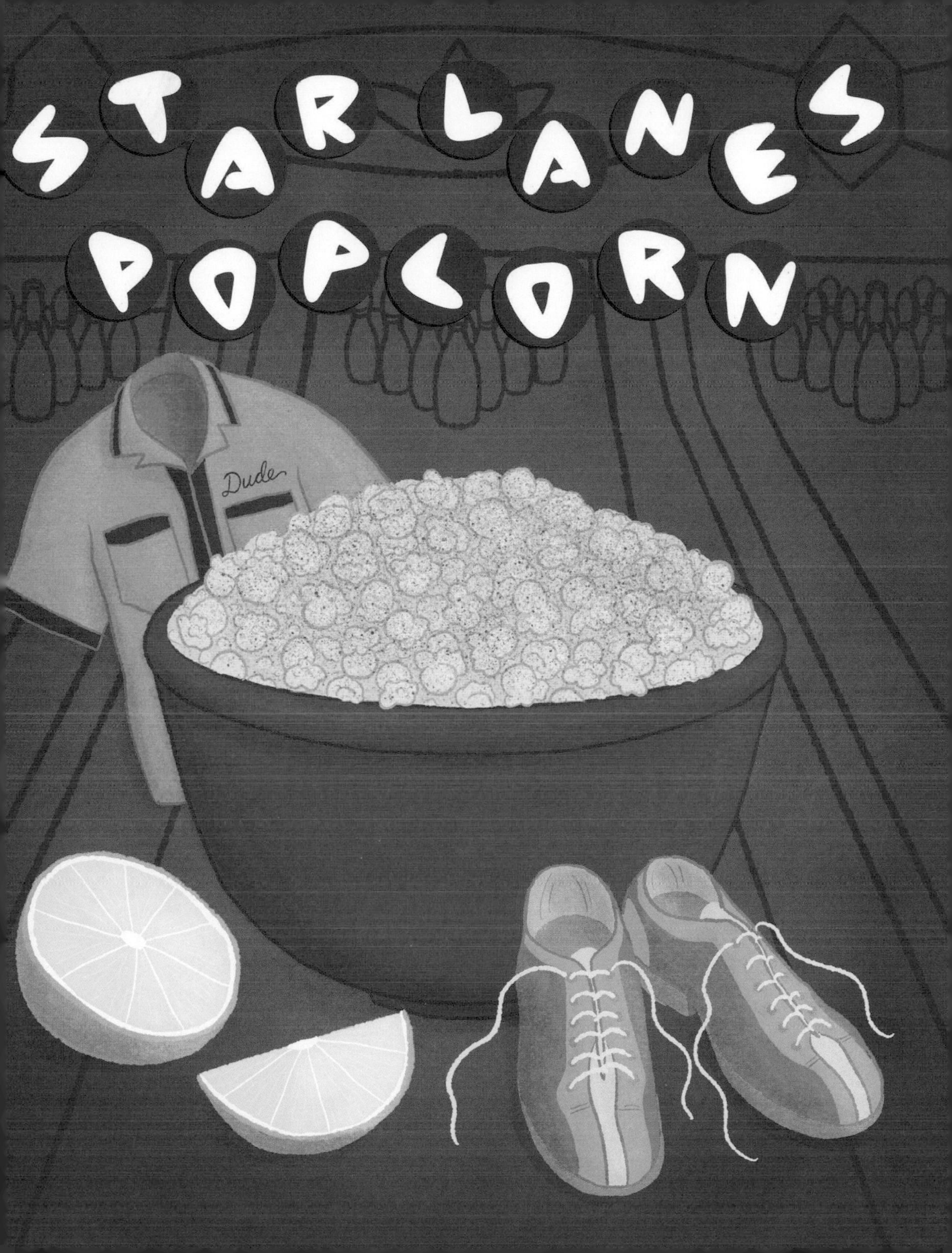
STARLANES
POPCORN
Dude

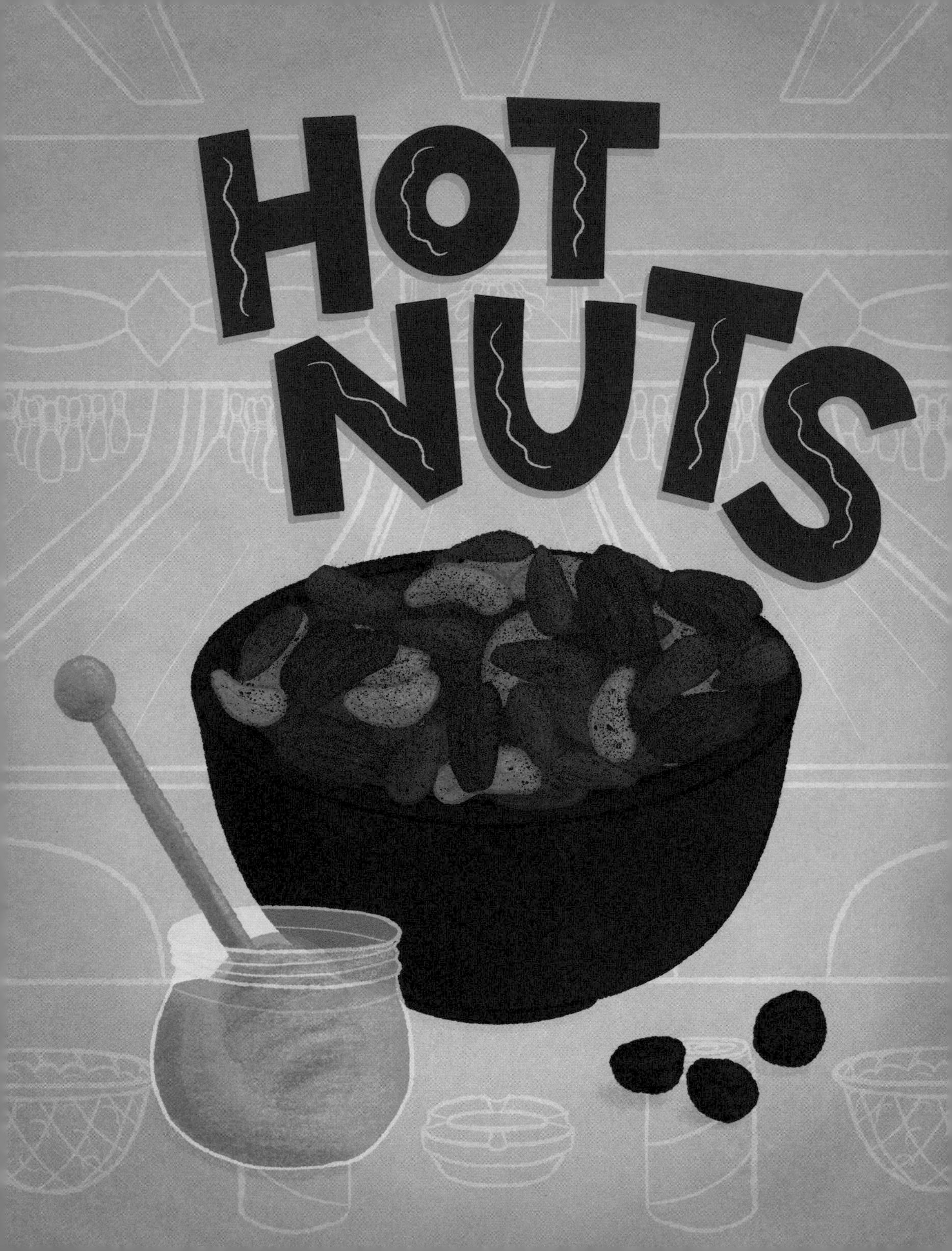
HOT
NUTS

# HOT NUTS

## *Serves 12*

Hot nuts are a bowling alley staple, and here they get a flavorful update with this coffee-glazed version that pairs perfectly with White Russians (as well as most other cocktails). Just a touch bitter, they act as the perfect contrast to mixed drinks that are on the sweeter side. Plus, talk about a buzz! Note that these nuts are best served warm, not hot, so that the glaze has a chance to cool and harden.

## INGREDIENTS

¼ cup (50 g) sugar

1 tablespoon honey

1 tablespoon ground coffee

1 teaspoon kosher salt

2 tablespoons water

4 cups (560 g) roasted unsalted mixed nuts

½ teaspoon vanilla extract

## DIRECTIONS

Preheat the oven to 350°F (175°C). Line a baking sheet with parchment paper or foil.

In a large saucepan over medium-high heat, combine the sugar, honey, ground coffee, salt, and water.

Bring to a boil, stirring constantly, until the sugar is dissolved.

Remove from the heat and add the nuts and vanilla, stirring until completely coated.

Spread the nut mixture in an even layer on the prepared baking sheet.

Bake for 5 minutes, then stir the nuts.

Bake for an additional 10 minutes, or until the coating hardens.

Remove from the oven and let cool slightly on the baking sheet before serving.

# DA JESUS SALAD

## *Serves 4 to 8*

As the character Jesus might say, don't flash your piece out on the lanes with this purple salad. This is all passion. It features a heady blend of beets, red onion, citrus, and spices, and it is here to f**k you up. These beets may even help you roll your way to the semis. Too tasty? Too interesting? Dios mío, man. Nobody messes with these beets.

## INGREDIENTS

2 tablespoons olive oil

2 tablespoons Worcestershire sauce

1 teaspoon kosher salt

¼ teaspoon ground black pepper

1½ pounds (680 g) small beets, scrubbed, stemmed, and quartered

¼ cup (35 g) minced red onion

2 tablespoons fresh lime juice

½ teaspoon paprika

⅛ teaspoon ground cumin

2 tablespoons chopped fresh cilantro

⅔ cup (60 g) crumbled queso fresco

## DIRECTIONS

Preheat the oven to 425°F (220°C).

In a medium bowl, combine the olive oil, Worcestershire sauce, salt, and pepper.

Add the beets and toss to coat.

Transfer the beets to a sheet pan or cookie sheet and roast for 35 to 40 minutes, turning once or twice, until tender.

Remove the beets from the oven and let cool.

In a large bowl, add the onion, lime juice, paprika, cumin, cilantro, and queso fresco.

Add the beets to this mixture and toss to combine.

# Lingonberry Pancakes

# LINGONBERRY PANCAKES

## *Serves 4*

When the Nihilists eat at the diner, one of them orders lingonberry pancakes. This must be no ordinary diner, because traditional Swedish pancakes are not like American ones at all; they're more akin to French crepes. Lingonberries are a cousin to blueberries, but they're red and tart. The jam is available in specialty grocery stores and online.

## INGREDIENTS

1 cup (125 g) all-purpose flour

2 tablespoons sugar

2 eggs

2 cups whole milk

6 tablespoons unsalted butter, softened, divided

¼ teaspoon kosher salt

Lingonberry preserves, for serving

## DIRECTIONS

In a blender, combine the flour, sugar, eggs, milk, 3 tablespoons of the butter, and salt and blend until smooth.

Let the mixture rest in the refrigerator for at least 2 hours.

In a small saucepan, melt the remaining 3 tablespoons butter over low heat to avoid burning.

Add a small drizzle of the melted butter to a medium nonstick skillet over medium-high heat.

Add ½ cup batter and swirl to coat the bottom of the skillet.

When bubbles appear on the surface, about 2 to 4 minutes, flip the pancake and cook an additional 2 minutes.

Transfer to a cutting board or plate and repeat until all pancakes are cooked.

Serve with lingonberry preserves.

*Dude Fact*

When we finally meet the Nihilist's girlfriend who sacrificed her toe, we see that the character is played by musician Aimee Mann.

# PIGS IN A BLANKET

## Makes 16

It's easy to miss, but when the Nihilists order food at the diner, one of them asks for pigs in a blanket. A venerable bit of Americana, the dish we know as pigs in a blanket first appeared on our shores in the Betty Crocker Cookbook in the late 1950s. The recipe likely hails from Germany—which may be why the Coen Brothers chose it (that, and it's hilarious). This version features an added dash of mustard and caraway. Both additions are optional, but work to combat life's meaninglessness with unique flavor.

## INGREDIENTS

1 can (8 ounces, or 227g) crescent roll dough

2 teaspoons Dijon mustard

16 mini hot dogs

1 tablespoon caraway seeds

### Dude Fact

In this scene, the Dude and Walter's van is visible through the diner window.

## DIRECTIONS

Preheat the oven to 375°F (190°C).

Cut the crescent roll dough into 16 triangles.

Smear the dough lightly with the mustard.

Place the hot dogs along the base (the shortest side) of each triangle and roll up in the dough.

Arrange on an ungreased cookie sheet and sprinkle with the caraway seeds.

Bake for 12 to 15 minutes, until the dough is browned and cooked through.

# Pigs in a Blanket

Mustard

Crescent Rolls

STARLANES NACHOS

BLACK BEANS

# STAR LANES NACHOS

## Serves 6

While most bowling alley versions are sad affairs sporting fake cheese kept warm under heat lamps, these league favorites pack serious flavor. The secret is blending a few chipotle peppers to make a sauce that really ties the dish together.

## INGREDIENTS

3 chipotle peppers in adobo sauce

½ teaspoon chili powder

½ teaspoon ground cumin

½ teaspoon garlic powder

½ teaspoon onion powder

¼ cup water

2 tablespoons fresh lime juice

1 can (15 ounces, or 425 g) black beans, drained and rinsed

1 bag (12 ounces, or 340 g) tortilla chips

2½ cups (285 g) grated sharp cheddar cheese

Sour cream, jalapeño slices, green onion, for serving (optional)

## DIRECTIONS

Preheat the oven to 375°F (190°C). Line a large baking sheet with foil.

In a food processor or blender, combine the chipotle peppers, chili powder, cumin, garlic powder, onion powder, water, and lime juice.

In a medium saucepan over medium heat, combine the black beans and chipotle mixture and let simmer until the liquid is almost absorbed, about 10 minutes.

Arrange half the tortilla chips and top with half the bean mixture and half the cheese. Repeat with the remaining beans and cheese.

Bake 10 to 12 minutes, until the cheese is melted and the chips are just browned.

Serve with sour cream, jalapeño slices, and green onion, if desired.

# AVOCADO LATKES

*Serves 4*

What's Polish, kosher, and Southern Californian? These latkes, which are a fantastic crowd-pleaser to soak up cocktails. Easy to prepare, latkes are just the thing when you've got a little party going but need something to eat, or if some Lebowskis have crashed on your couch and you need to prepare something in the morning for the hangovers.

## AVOCADO DIPPING SAUCE

1 ripe avocado

1 ounce fresh lime juice

1 tablespoon minced fresh cilantro

¼ teaspoon kosher salt

## LATKES

5 medium russet potatoes, peeled

1 white onion

3 eggs

½ cup (65 g) cornstarch

½ teaspoon kosher salt
¼ cup peanut oil

## DIRECTIONS

To make the avocado dipping sauce: In a food processor or small bowl, combine the avocado, lime juice, cilantro, and salt and pulse or mash until smooth.

To make the latkes: With a box grater, grate the potatoes and onion.

Using a cheesecloth, squeeze out the excess liquid in the mixture.

In a large bowl, combine the eggs, cornstarch, and salt.

Add the potato and onion mixture and stir to combine.

Using a ¼-cup measuring cup, scoop the mixture and form it into roughly 4-inch (10 cm) patties.

In a large skillet over medium-high heat, heat the oil until it is hot but not smoking.

Working in batches, add the patties to the hot oil and fry until both sides are golden brown.

Transfer to a wire rack to drain.

# MEAT JOY

## *Makes 12 meatballs*

Maude Lebowski is purportedly based on the 1970s avant-garde artist Carolee Schneemann, who, among other things, is famous for a performance work called "Meat Joy." Serve these high-brow-meets-low-brow meatballs with a version of the famed In-N-Out Burger sauce for an addictive go-to for parties. The secret to their success is seasoned bread crumbs, which mimic the flavor experience of a burger.

## IN-N-OUT SAUCE

½ cup mayonnaise

¼ cup ketchup

2 tablespoons sweet pickle relish

1 teaspoon sugar

1 teaspoon distilled white vinegar

2 dashes Worcestershire sauce

## INGREDIENTS

1 pound (454 g) ground beef

1 egg

½ cup (50 g) seasoned bread crumbs

2 tablespoons ketchup

1 teaspoon onion powder

½ teaspoon kosher salt

½ teaspoon ground black pepper

1 tablespoon unsalted butter

## DIRECTIONS

To make the In-N-Out sauce: In a medium bowl, stir the ingredients until combined.

To make the meatballs: Preheat the oven to 350°F (175°C).

In a large bowl, combine the ground beef, egg, bread crumbs, ketchup, onion powder, salt, and pepper. Mix until combined.

Form the mixture into meatballs about the size of a golf ball, 2 inches (4 to 5 cm) in size. Heat a large oven-safe skillet medium heat.

Add the butter and swirl in the pan to coat.

Add the meatballs in a single layer and brown on all sides, turning constantly. Cook for 5 minutes.

Transfer the skillet to the oven cook for an additional 8 minutes.

Remove from oven and serve with In-N-Out Sauce.

# LOGJAMMERS

*Serves 4*

Grab the syrup, it's time for logjammin'! Just try to resist these long, thick trunks. Whether you're waiting for a handyman to fix your cable or for a friend to drop by to use the shower, these delicious logs are a treat for everyone. Best of all? You can use your fingers.

## INGREDIENTS

6 thick slices stale bread, crust removed

3 eggs

3 cups whole milk

1 teaspoon vanilla extract

¼ cup (50 g) sugar

1 tablespoon ground cinnamon

4 tablespoons unsalted butter, divided

Maple syrup, for serving (optional)

## DIRECTIONS

Cut each bread slice into 3 even, thick strips.

In a shallow bowl, combine the eggs, milk, and vanilla.

In a separate shallow bowl or on a plate, combine the sugar and cinnamon.

Melt 2 tablespoons of the butter in a large skillet over medium-low heat.

Working in batches and using tongs, soak the bread in the egg mixture and then dip in the sugar mixture, coating on all sides.

Cook the breadsticks until golden brown on all sides, adding more butter when needed.

Serve with maple syrup, if desired.

# PARLEZ-USTED INGLÉS

## *Serves 4*

Although obviously so educated that he sponsors higher education for inner-city youth, the Big Lebowski nevertheless would flunk both a French and Spanish exam. He attempts to inquire if the Dude speaks English by asking, "Parlez-usted inglés?" This eponymously named French-meets-Spanish-meets-English dessert is a true cross-cultural delight. While not exactly a custard (it doesn't contain eggs), this light and easy version will find its way into your regular dessert rotation.

## INGREDIENTS

3 cups whole milk

½ cup (100 g) sugar

¼ cup (30 g) cornstarch

1 teaspoon vanilla extract

⅛ teaspoon ground cinnamon

## DIRECTIONS

In a medium saucepan over medium heat, heat the milk until just beginning to steam.

Slowly add the sugar, cornstarch, vanilla, and cinnamon. Stir until the sugar dissolves, the ingredients are combined, and the mixture is smooth.

Reduce the heat to medium-low and continue to stir until the sauce begins to thicken and coats the back of the spoon.

Remove from heat and transfer to a large bowl or individual ramekins (makes four 4-ounce ramekins). Cover with a kitchen towel and let cool on the counter for 30 minutes.

Transfer to the refrigerator and chill for at least 2 hours before serving.

# LITTLE LEBOWSKIS

## *Serves 4*

There's a Little Lebowski on the way! The Stranger (Sam Elliott) tells us the news after Donny dies in order to comfort us. It is, as he says, "the way the whole darned human comedy keeps perpetuatin' itself." These Kahlúa-laced blondies are sadly not self-perpetuating, so you'll have to whip up a batch every time you want them—but it's a snap. Perfect for gatherings, any ol' Tuesday night, or baby showers.

## INGREDIENTS

½ cup (115 g) unsalted butter, melted

1 cup (220 g) light brown sugar

1 egg

1 teaspoon vanilla extract

½ cup Kahlúa

1¼ cups (155 g) all-purpose flour

½ teaspoon kosher salt

## DIRECTIONS

Preheat the oven to 350°F (175°C) and grease a 9-inch square baking pan.

In a medium bowl, mix the melted butter and sugar until combined.

Add the egg, vanilla, and Kahlúa and stir to combine.

In a separate medium bowl, combine the flour and salt.

Very slowly incorporate the dry ingredients into the wet ingredients and mix to combine thoroughly.

Transfer the mixture to the prepared pan.

Bake for 25 to 30 minutes, until a toothpick inserted in the middle comes out clean. Let set and cool completely before serving.

little lebowskis

## BUNNY'S POOL PARTY

This lazy pool party is inspired by Bunny herself. Under the hot summer's sun, put on your bathing suit and get your guests in the pool! Pull out the beach loungers and pool inflatables, gather your favorite nail polish color, and grab a glass of something bubbly. Take the day to relax as Bunny would (at least how she usually would when we can find her). Disclaimer: any video cameras brought are at your own risk.

### FOOD MENU

Pigs in a Blanket 152

Star Lanes Popcorn 144

Hot Nuts 146

Avocado Latkes 156

### BOOZE MENU

Where's Bunny? 32

Karl Hungus 42

Porn Star Martini 90

The Nihilist 104

The Knutsons 118

*Album Paring*
SPICE
by Spice Girls

## MEMORIAL PICNIC FOR DONNY

Even though Walter would often cut off whatever it was Donny was saying, Donny's untimely heart attack leaves an absence behind just the same. But let's not make remembering this beloved character a sad occasion. To honor Donny Kerabatsos, plan a memorial picnic on a cliffside overlooking the sea. Go around telling walrus jokes and wear your favorite solid-colored polo shirt to exude the essence of this quirky character. Don't forget to bring a can of Folgers coffee!

### FOOD MENU

Da Jesus Salad 148

Meat Joy 158

Little Lebowskis 164

### BOOZE MENU

The Kerabatsos 46

I Am the Walrus 52

Modestly Priced Receptacle 86

*Album Paring*
PROCOL HARUM
by Procol Harum

## VENICE BEACH BOWLING TEAM PARTY

Transform a standard bowling game into a hippie, desert-themed party commemorating the Dude and his friends of the Venice Beach bowling team. In their honor, bring your favorite people to the lanes in your best '90s outfits to match those timeless bowling shoes. Throw some rugs on the floor to tie it all together.

### FOOD MENU

Star Lanes Popcorn 144

Star Lanes Nachos 154

Pigs in a Blanket 152

*Album Pairing*
ESCAPE
by Journey

### BOOZE MENU

Sarsaparilla 36

Let's Go Bowling 44

Venice Beach League 58

Star Lanes 96

## MURDER MYSTERY PARTY: WHO HAS THE MONEY?

Survive the night and find the culprit who has the briefcase holding a million dollars. Is it Maude, Donny, Jesus, Karl Hungus, or Larry Sellers? The risk is spiked drinks, smashed car windows, and ferrets in the bathtub. Will you find the money, or will you lose a toe for joining the wrong side?

### FOOD MENU

Avocado Latkes 156

Meat Joy 158

Parlez-Usted Inglés 162

### BOOZE MENU

Urban Achievers 56

Stranger in the Alps 78

Chinstrap 82

*Album Pairing*
THE DARK SIDE OF THE MOON
by Pink Floyd

# MARTY'S AFTER-PARTY

Whether it's for a sold-out show or the reenactment of the portrait of Mussorgsky, a swanky after-party will make anyone's night end with a bang. For a best friend, landlord, or an ex-wife's Pomeranian who didn't place first in the Best Dog show, create invites in the format of a playbill and be sure to put in the dress code that it's a black-tie event. Soon, everyone will be able to forget what happened onstage.

## FOOD MENU

Da Jesus Salad 148

Lingonberry Pancakes 150

Little Lebowskis 164

## BOOZE MENU

Dance Quintet 48

His Dudeness 134

Tender Resignation 110

Bums Always Lose 124

*Album Pairing*
*BIG SCIENCE*
by Laurie Anderson

# A TREEHORN GARDEN PARTY

Take your garden party to the next level as if porn producer Jackie Treehorn is paying for it. This avant-garde summer night's party, equipped with a pool, well-kept gardens, and fancy cocktail dress, will be a night no one will forget. Disclaimer: No drinks will be spiked unless you owe the host an outstanding debt.

## FOOD MENU

Avocado Latkes 156

Da Jesus Salad 148

Logjammers 160

Hot Nuts 146

## BOOZE MENU

Stay Out of Malibu 80

Treehorn 84

Moonless Prairie Night 122

Feed the Monkey 94

*Album Pairing*
*EXOTICA*
by Martin Denny

## PAINTING NIGHT WITH MAUDE

Turn a quaint painting night into one extravagant enough that Maude would host it. With the room blasting sensual or inspirational music, and everyone wearing green smocks akin to Maude's infamous cape, let the cocktails flow and the creativity soar. If you happen to have access to a zip line, I'm sure she'd appreciate that, too. The option of clothing will be at the host's discretion.

### FOOD MENU

Meat Joy 158

Little Lebowskis 164

### BOOZE MENU

Knox Harrington 40

Maude's Manhattan 108

Nagelbett 116

Young Jeffrey 138

*Album Pairing*
*TAKING TIGER MOUNTAIN (BY STRATEGY)*
by Brian Eno

## A LAZY DUDE GATHERING

Take the chill vibes of the Dude, the laziest person in the world, as inspiration for a low-stakes, quintessential hang-out. Gather your friends to spend a lazy day with psychedelic music and White Russians, with no pressure to dance, talk, or even get up from the couch. No ferrets or rug pissers are allowed.

### FOOD MENU

Star Lanes Nachos 154

Logjammers 160

Lingonberry Pancakes 150

### BOOZE MENU

Tumbleweed 30

Ransom Courier 64

Occasional Acid Flashback 66

Tai the Room Together 70

The Dude 132

*Album Pairing*
*ELECTRIC LADYLAND*
by Jimi Hendrix

# ACKNOWLEDGMENTS

I can now die with a smile on my face without feeling like the Good Lord cheated me. Because, in all my years of writing, I have never had quite as much fun as I did working on *The Unofficial Big Lebowski Cocktail Book*. A big thank-you to editor Cara Donaldson for the chance to channel my inner Dude and also to my agent, Clare Pelino, who is wise and abides. Likewise, a big shout-out to Kevin Lundell of Broad Street Beverage Co., who helped recipe test the cocktails in this book. Finally, a gigantic thank-you to my bowling partner in life and special lady, Janine Hawley.

# ABOUT THE AUTHOR

André Darlington is the author of nine cocktail books, including *Bar Menu and Gotham City Cocktails: Official Handcrafted Food & Drinks From the World of Batman*. He lives as casually as possible in North Carolina.

# INDEX

Brimming with creative inspiration, how-to projects, and useful information to enrich your everyday life, quarto.com is a favorite destination for those pursuing their interests and passions.

© 2023 by Quarto Publishing Group USA Inc.
Text © 2023 by André G. Darlington

First published in 2023 by Epic Ink, an imprint of The Quarto Group,
142 West 36th Street, 4th Floor, New York, NY 10018, USA
T (212) 779-4972  F (212) 779-6058  www.Quarto.com

Epic Ink titles are also available at discount for retail, wholesale, promotional, and bulk purchase. For details, contact the Special Sales Manager by email at specialsales@quarto.com or by mail at The Quarto Group, Attn: Special Sales Manager, 100 Cummings Center Suite 265D, Beverly, MA 01915 USA.

10 9 8 7 6 5 4 3 2 1

ISBN: 978-0-7603-8121-2

Library of Congress Control Number: 2022943935

Publisher: Rage Kindelsperger
Creative Director: Laura Drew
Managing Editor: Cara Donaldson
Editorial Assistant: Katelynn Abraham
Interior Design: Laura Drew and Beth Middleworth
Layout Design: Beth Middleworth
Cover and Interior Illustrations: Jennifer Hines

Printed in China